COSMIC WIZARD

A JOURNEY FROM OUTER RAGE TO INNER SAGE

Jeff Anthony

COSMIC WIZARD

Copyright© 2017 by Jeff Anthony

Disclaimer:

The views expressed by the author in reference to specific people in their book represent entirely their own individual opinions and are not in any way reflective of the views of Transformation Catalyst Books, LLC. We assume no responsibility for errors, omissions or contradictory interpretation of the subject matter herein.

Transformation Catalyst Books, LLC does not warrant the performance, effectiveness, or applicability of any websites listed in or linked to this publication. The purchaser or reader of this publication assumes responsibility of the use of these materials and information. Transformation Catalyst Books, LLC shall in no event be held liable to any party for any direct, indirect, punitive, special, incidental, or any other consequential damages arising directly or indirectly from any use of this material. Techniques and processes given in this book are not to be used in place of medical or other professional advice.

No part of this book may be reproduced or transmitted in any form, or by any means, electronic or mechanical, including photography, recording, or in any information storage or retrieval system without written permission from the author or publisher, except in the case of brief quotations embodied in articles and reviews.

Published by:
Transformation Books
211 Pauline Drive #513
York, PA 17402
www.TransformationBooks.com

ISBN # 978-1-945252-25-9
Library of Congress Control No: 2017935998

Cover Design: Jeff Anthony
Layout and typesetting: Ranilo Cabo
Editor: Allison Saia
Proofreader: Gwen Hoggnagle
Midwife: Carrie Jareed

Printed in the United States of America

To Dad

TABLE OF CONTENTS

Introduction 1

Chapter 1: Hondo, Texas 5
Chapter 2: Happy Birthday 17
Chapter 3: Out-Processed 31
Chapter 4: Nowhere to Turn 39
Chapter 5: Lost in a Fog 55
Chapter 6: Adjustment Disorder 65
Chapter 7: Shoving Off 77
Chapter 8: Cold Shower 85
Chapter 9: Are You Happy? 93
Chapter 10: Shattered 101
Chapter 11: My Muse 115
Chapter 12: The Golden Vine 127
Chapter 13: Soul Flight 141
Chapter 14: An Open Mind 155
Chapter 15: Grasshopper 167
Chapter 16: Unmasked 183
Chapter 17: Find Your Smile 197
Chapter 18: Harmony 209

Acknowledgments 219
About the Author 221

INTRODUCTION

There was a time in my life when I looked to the outside world to try and fix my problems, make me happy, or cure my illness. I was living in my head, racing through life at breakneck speed trying to figure it all out, all the while attempting to have a "normal" life, never realizing that life was all around me, fighting to get in. I spent much of my life raging against things that had already happened, blind to my potential. Sometimes we just need to get out of our own way.

From the time we're born, we're being programmed. We're taught to operate in a world that resembles the one that programmed us. Culture, politics, parenting, and ideologies are the belief systems uploaded by well-meaning friends and family. We soon develop our own perspectives of right and wrong, possible and impossible, from these beliefs that we are expected to align with. The problem with this model is that a system, no matter how well intended, is limiting. These limiting beliefs about ourselves and our world form a matrix that binds us to the past and places limits on our future.

You've probably heard a parent say something like, "I sounded exactly like my mother! I swore I'd never say that to my kids." Our programmed belief systems are running automatically, reproducing exactly the outcome we wished to be free of as children. This can be frustrating for us and those around us, especially in unstable or chaotic households. When the beliefs about ourselves aren't our own, but somehow become our *modus operandi*, then we are trapped.

In our society we allow others to label us and define our experiences. They tell us who and what we are. After a while, through reinforcement, we become the things that our culture has convinced us to be. In my case, I allowed others to create a monster full of rage and anger because I chose to believe the things that others said about me, not knowing that I had the power to overcome my cultural limitations. The big problems arose when the same people who created this monster wanted to kill him through judgments and negativity. In other words, our culture labels us, and we allow these labels to define us, making them the truth of who and what we are.

For example, if we tell children often enough that they are stupid, angry, and volatile, they will create their lives to resemble rage-filled struggles. Through no fault of their own other than believing in society's feedback, they grow up to fulfill that destiny. They react violently or inappropriately to things they perceive as threatening to them, withdraw from society, and view themselves as separate or different, judging and blaming everything outside of their narrow viewpoint as wrong or flawed. To these people the world is a scary place divided by people of different cultures, races, and beliefs who are all out to get them.

On the other hand, children who are raised to cultivate an attitude of personal value and appreciation most often become valuable members of society with empathy and gratitude for the diversity of cultural expressions around them. They appreciate and accept others for the gifts they bring to their world.

Many of my personal struggles stemmed from an innocent belief in the things my culture convinced me to be. Years of conditioning had such a dramatic effect on my life that my concepts of right and wrong, good and bad, were skewed to the point that my subconscious beliefs and judgments sabotaged efforts to achieve my goals and change my life.

Once I realized what was going on, I was met with a choice. Continue on the path of self-limiting beliefs and stay in the projected failure-loop waiting for someone to rescue me while I raged against my angry world, or take the inner journey and become the hero of my own story.

CHAPTER 1

Hondo, Texas

My story begins with a couple of baby-boomers from Houston, Texas, otherwise known as my parents. Let's start with Dad, the only child of a hardened Navy chief who went on to become a mechanic, and later a teacher at the local prison in my hometown. His parents were overly critical and handed out daily doses of physical, verbal, and mental abuse. As a child he played baseball well enough to earn a college scholarship, yet his parents never watched him play a single game. They couldn't care less about his recreational activities or childhood friendships, and believed that he should worry about school, what they said, and nothing more. He was secluded from the outside world and deprived of a normal childhood.

When Dad was in elementary school, his father transferred from Hawaii to California. Everything seemed so different to him there, including the people. With his limited life experiences, he had never met a black man until his father introduced him to a black colleague. Being very curious, as any young child would be, he took an interest in the man's hands. Dad noticed that his hands were darker on the backs than on the palms. To him it seemed that the color had rubbed off.

When the man bent down to shake his hand, he shook it firmly, looked at his palm, and said to his father, "Look, Dad! My hand is still white. The color didn't rub off!"

Without a word of warning, his father struck him in the face with the back of his clenched hand. When the blow knocked Dad to the floor, his father said, "Get up and stop crying. Don't you ever let me hear you say anything like that again!" He couldn't understand that this was a new experience for my father and a rational conclusion for a seven-year-old kid to make.

Dad's father never took the time, nor did he have the patience required, to nurture and raise an opened-minded son. As he grew up, Dad succumbed to his parents' programming and became trapped in the same irrational, reactionary loop. He lacked the compassion he longed for as a child, soon becoming the rage-filled monster that his parents raised him to be.

At age twenty-two, Dad watched his abusive father die of a heart attack on Thanksgiving Day, soon followed by his mother's death from cancer only six months later. His only family, though unkind and unsupportive, were gone. Anger became his companion in life, guiding him through the cruel and unfair world. His discontent fueled his aggression, and fed his belief that "might is right." By holding on to his parents' belief systems, even after their deaths, Dad only further isolated himself emotionally and socially.

Mom is the second oldest of five children. Her mother was married to an abusive alcoholic whom she divorced only to marry yet another abusive alcoholic. Eventually, due to developmental issues and family problems, my mother was sent to live with her uncle and his wife. Mom loved her uncle dearly, and he cherished her, not having children of his own. Everything was better for a couple of years until she was thirteen and her uncle died suddenly of a heart attack. She spent another year alone with her aunt, who turned into a hollow shell, unable to give my mother love or attention. Then Mom returned home to live with her mother and finish school. Some years later she met the man of her dreams, and they decided to join their crazy worlds together and get married.

This is where I enter the story. Well, technically, my brother entered the story first, then me, and finally my sister. We were all born within two years of each other and with the same first letter in our names. (Having children close together and naming them in this way were both popular conventions in the '70s.)

In 1975 my parents settled forty-four miles south of San Antonio, Texas, in a small farm and ranch community called Hondo. This small town has just the basics: a couple of grocery stores, two gas stations, BBQ joints, a steakhouse, plenty of Mexican food, a volunteer fire department, more cows than people, and the pride and joy of the community – a good high school football team. Oh, and let's not forget the famous sign that greets highway travelers as they roll into town:

HONDO, TEXAS

WELCOME TO GOD'S COUNTRY PLEASE DON'T DRIVE THROUGH IT LIKE HELL

It's a breeding ground for Texas tough guys. If you weren't playing football, you were hunting, fishing, shooting guns, riding horses, racing motorcycles, or hauling hay to stay in shape for football season. In a place like this, everybody was looking to prove themselves. My brother was the superior student athlete, and my sister was into studying hard to prove her intellect. To define my role in the family, I mostly got into trouble and received the wrath of an angry father who licked his wounds by lashing out at me.

Before I was out of diapers, my father had already labeled me "the problem child." In typical tough-guy fashion, he never offered loving support or an encouraging embrace when I got hurt, needed help, or faced a challenge. Instead, it was verbal abuse followed by a beating. When he did speak to me, it was to throw out criticism and insults. I can't remember his ever saying "I love you," but I was referred to as "stupid" or a "piece of shit" on a regular basis.

Coming home from school one day, Dad greeted

me just as I came through the back door. My recent report card in his hand was a bad sign. "Look at this shit! What are you, stupid? Keep it up and your life's gonna be shit!" he yelled, the anger causing his face to swell up and turn bright red. Then he unbuckled his belt and I got my ass whipped over a couple of Cs on my report card.

Dinner at my house did not consist of funny stories and pleasant conversation as in most small-town homes. Table manners were a minefield of potentially explosive consequences, and everyone was always on high alert. Put your elbows on the table or speak with your mouth full, and Dad would launch his atomic attack. One evening I was excited to add to my brother's story about after-school baseball practice, but the words came flying out of my mouth along with a forgotten piece of food. Dad shoved back his chair to interrupt the story and taught me about table manners by throwing my plate on the floor while simultaneously grabbing my hair and forcing me to the ground. "If you're gonna eat like a dog then you're gonna eat with the dog!" he barked down at me, spit flying through his teeth.

Mom stayed in her seat and made a futile attempt to help. "Uhh... I don't think you should..." A piercing

glare from Dad cut her off short.

I crouched on my hands and knees, watching through welled-up tears of demoralization as the dog devoured my dinner. My family continued to eat in silence. My brother opened his mouth only to shovel in his food and didn't dare to share any more of his day. When everyone, including the dog, was done eating, Dad bellowed from the table, "Now get on your feet and clean this mess up." I watched my family walk out of the room, their shoulders slumped like a funeral procession, as I carefully scraped the remaining food off the floor. This debilitating, inhumane treatment seared my young mind with the brand of rage.

Amid the turbulence and chaos of our home, at least I had my brother to lean on. We spent a lot of time together exploring and playing with our BB guns. Trying to shoot each other was part of the fun. One sultry summer afternoon in front of our trailer, my brother shot me with his BB gun, so I turned around and shot him back. I nailed him right in the butt, and doubled over with laughter as his arms flailed and he grabbed his backside.

I froze when I saw Dad's truck and heard his voice booming from the open window, "You boys better get

your asses inside!" Leaping out of the pickup truck, he grabbed me by the shirt and picked me up off the ground. He dragged me into the house, while yelling and screaming profanely, then paused to warn my brother, "You'll be next!"

Dad tossed me into the living room and grabbed a large, thick wooden paddle that he had sculpted at work, specifically crafted for handing out discipline. "Grab your ankles, and if you let go we're starting over!" He cocked back his arm and unloaded on me like a thunderstorm on a hot Texas night. Of course I let go, and we had to start over. I don't know how far into the beating we were when I heard "Crack!" and the paddle splintered across my backside.

I turned to see my brother standing there in shock, his face wet with tears. Dad grabbed me by the shirt and lifted me off the ground. "Don't you ever point a gun at anybody again. Now get out of my face, you fucking crybaby!"

He then turned to my brother. "You, too. Get outta here! You can thank your brother for breaking the paddle; it's your lucky day."

My brother was eleven years old and I was nine.

Three years later, on an oppressively hot August afternoon, Mom sent me to get my brother from a

friend's house. It was a long walk, and I was a little irritated with the task. When I arrived, I knocked on the door. "Go away!" the boys yelled from inside. I kept banging on the flapping screen door of the double-wide trailer until my brother and his friend appeared around the corner with a high-powered air rifle for hunting small game.

"How 'bout now! You gonna go now?" his friend threatened, aiming the rifle at me.

"Come on, stop jerking around and let's go!" I said.

I guess I realized he wasn't jerking around when I saw a blast of air exiting the barrel of the rifle and "Boom!" – my chest was transformed into a bloody mess.

I went down in a heap, and the boys came running. Being from Texas, we'd seen too many Western films. My brother and his friend logically applied Jack Daniels whiskey to the wound. Their next surgical procedure was to cut away all of the stringy fat hanging out of the wound with kitchen scissors. After applying more whiskey and lots of pressure, the bleeding subsided. They bandaged me up and my brother and I set off for the house. My brother easily convinced me that Dad would kill the both of us, and made me promise not to tell our parents. Even though my health was at risk, I never said a word.

Somehow I always found a way to get Dad's attention no matter how hard I tried to avoid it. One summer afternoon of my freshman year, I went into San Antonio with my brother and his friend just to walk around the mall. We contorted our large bodies to squeeze into my brother's tiny 1979 Honda hatchback and took off for the city. At a strip mall, we burst out of the little car like a group of circus clowns. The searing summer heat was rising off the blacktop parking lot, and we wandered into a department store, mostly to escape the oven-like conditions outside.

We were in the store for maybe ten minutes before my brother and his friend started egging me on to steal something. I had never stolen anything in my life, but with enough razzing and punches in the arm followed by expletives, I gave in and tried my hand at shoplifting. As you would expect, I got caught. My day of fun came to a screeching halt. Mom had to drive into town from my grandparents' ranch, so everyone in the family found out about the incident and was equally disappointed and judgmental.

The security officers released me into the custody of my mother. She was surprisingly quiet on the drive home, probably praying in silence that Dad wouldn't kill me. When the tires of the car touched our driveway, the gate to the backyard flew open and Dad overtook the driver's seat. I tried to jump out of the car but he dragged me back in. Locked and loaded, he proceeded to backhand me repeatedly on our commute to the local video store. He pulled up, got out, dropped the videos in the slot, got back in, and recommenced the assault. The abuse ended where it began, in our driveway, only now I was bleeding from the nose and mouth and had a puffy left eye.

The beating was followed by a long, arduous evening filled with psychological abuse and profanity-laced lectures. "I'm embarrassed to have you as a son!" Dad said. "Now your grandparents and everyone else knows what a little shithead you are!"

He never mentioned that stealing is wrong or offered fatherly advice about the incident. He only seemed to care about the embarrassment to the family and the fact that my Mom had to pick my ass up. Mom never mentioned that day or acknowledged any of the abuse she witnessed. I realized that I was alone in this battle and needed an escape plan.

I learned to hide the painful parts of my life and "suck it up." That's what real men do; they never

cry or show emotions, and they keep painful secrets. They only tell the selective truth. You know what I mean – select which truth is going to keep you out of trouble because lying is wrong. The other lesson Dad taught me was "If you're going to do something wrong, don't get caught.

During my last grueling year at home my brother came to visit from college and offered me some advice. "Maybe you should join the military," he said. "You've already let Mom and Dad down enough. I mean, you know you aren't ready for college."

He was right, and I actually listened because I wanted out so badly that I could taste it. More than that, I wanted to prove myself and redeem the respect that I'd lost. "You know, you're right. I'll make them all proud of me. I'll join the Navy."

CHAPTER 2

Happy Birthday

I felt like a wild animal released from his cage as I exited the plane in San Diego. I was a little sad to leave Mom and my sister, but I only had feelings of relief about escaping Dad's tyranny. However, my plan did not go as smoothly as I had hoped. When I arrived at the base for boot camp, I quickly realized that I had jumped into another psychological operation where people would be testing me. I was up to the challenge though, because I'd been battle tested at home. After growing up in "Texas tough-guy land" with a dad who had an iron will and fists like battering rams, I was well seasoned.

The name of my company was The Devil Dogs, and I made it my mission to be the most devilish dog of them all. The first two guys selected to lead our company were mentally weak and lacked leadership skills. In the first week the company's morale was low after failed inspections and overall poor performance. That weekend, after being one of the few recruits to take no hits on inspection, I asked the chief in charge of my company if I could take over. "What, Anthony, you think you can turn this thing around and lead these recruits?" he asked.

"Sir, I know I can!" I proudly responded. I was out to prove myself, and leading a company of 120 men was just my cup of tea. My company ended up graduating boot camp as one of the Honor Guard companies. I never took a single hit on any of the inspections and scored 100 percent on all my physical and academic testing. I graduated number one out of 1,200 men.

The next duty station for me was Naval Firefighter Training on Treasure Island, just across the bay from San Francisco. I was awarded advancements in rank and pay grade for my performance in boot camp. Then I was asked to lead the firefighting recruits and be the dorm monitor, all of which I was more than happy to do.

I studied hard, listened to instructions, and again took zero hits on inspections. This time I graduated number two out of about 1,500 students. Things were going great. No one could question that I was proving myself now! Due to my diligence I received another bump in rank and pay grade, and got to pick where I wanted my next duty station to be. I selected a precommissioned ship, which means the ship was still under construction. The guided missile destroyer was being assembled in Pascagoula, Mississippi. I had the unique opportunity to learn more about the ship's systems than most of the other new firefighters in the Navy. We helped install the systems and bring them online for the first time.

I used this time to learn as much as I could. It was fun work, and the people on the ship took an interest in me. In just eighteen months I had climbed the ranks of the military from E1 to E4 and had gone from making $880 a month to $1,600 a month. This was usually only accomplished after four years in the military, and would be like starting your freshman year of high school and graduating eighteen months later. Now all of my hard work was paying off. I was getting noticed and treated with respect. Shortly after making rank and pay grade, my lieutenant came to me and asked, "What's a smart kid like you doing in the enlisted service? You should be an officer."

He told me I could be released and receive a college degree on the military's nickel. All I had to do was re-up for six years after college. It sounded like a good plan to me – free college and a guaranteed job afterward. He handed me a folder full of forms to fill out to apply for the Officer Training Program. I was being offered a free education and a major advancement over my current enlisted status. This sort of treatment was new to me. I had never known encouragement from my Dad, and I was eating it up.

Amid the excitement I started to notice something disconcerting about myself. The first thing was that even though I was doing well, receiving awards, gaining advancements, and earning bigger paychecks, I was miserable and depressed. Full of resentment and anger, I was using these emotions to fuel my success. Hatred towards Dad burned inside of me. This rage drove my formula for success.

The second and more immediate concern was that I had never felt quite right, physically, since boot camp. I started to have severe muscle and joint pain, primarily in my legs. They fatigued quickly and took longer and longer to recuperate each time I exercised. Then one day we went out for our required physical training test, and I failed the mile run. I couldn't even finish it in under nine minutes. Before that I could have run it in just over five. No matter how hard I tried, I couldn't get my legs to respond. It felt as if I was dragging a couple of refrigerators through sand, like dead weight, and I had no energy. Due to my excellent physical performances on previous tests, it was excused or overlooked.

Scared and confused, I thought to myself, *What the hell is going on with me, and who can I turn to?* Remember, I'm a Texas tough guy who can suck it up. I convinced myself it was no big deal and that I'd go see the doc in a week or so. But soon I had shooting pains in my feet, ankles, and knees. Just walking around was painful, so to the doc I went.

The doc had me show him where the pain was, gave me some ibuprofen, and sent me on my way. He tried to console me. "Anthony, you're a big, strong boy, and I'm sure your body's just adjusting to ship life. These steel decks can be tough on the leg joints. You'll be fine."

The pain continued for a few months and increased over time. I repeatedly went to the medical staff and complained about leg pains and low energy

levels. The problem was that I had a reputation as a tough guy, and no one would listen to me or believe me. I felt trapped in a prison of my own design, but I kept doing my job and sucking it up. *Surely a doctor knows more than I do, right? After all, they're the experts!*

After more than a year of frustration, my best friend Rob, who was in the Air Force, had a great idea. "If none of the people on your ship will listen to you, then why don't you just go to the Air Force base and see one of the docs there."

The next weekend I took his advice. It was a dreary October morning on the Gulf Coast as I made my way to the walk-in area of the Keesler Medical Facility. I nervously waited a short while before they called my name. A young second lieutenant walked me back to the exam room, asked some basic questions, and gave me a physical.

He was impressed with my physical appearance and couldn't see anything of immediate concern, so I said, "You see, that's the problem! I look fit, so nobody will listen to me!"

I must have sounded distraught because the second lieutenant shifted to a consoling voice and asked, "Has anyone ordered a blood analysis? Maybe you have mono or something?"

HAPPY BIRTHDAY

He took some blood and I went back to the ship, relieved that someone was finally listening to me. The young doctor had given me hope when he assessed the situation and guessed it was something minor. I hung out with friends the rest of the day and had pretty much dismissed my concerns by the time I hit the rack (went to bed). *Why have I been so concerned over something like mono?* I thought just before I fell asleep.

A shipmate frantically shook me awake a few hours later. "Why are you waking me up? It's three o'clock in the morning," I complained.

"You have an urgent phone call on the main deck!" the young boatswain's mate informed me.

Tired and confused, I had forgotten about my appointment the previous day in Biloxi. Walking up to the main deck on that dark, ominous morning, I wondered what had happened. Usually when someone received a phone call in the middle of the night it was serious. I worried that something bad had happened to a family member. As I angled the phone towards my ear, expecting the worst, I heard a familiar voice. It was the doctor from the day before.

"Are you feeling okay right now?"

"Yes, Sir. I feel fine."

"Are you sitting down?"

"No."

"Why don't you grab a seat and let me explain a few things," he said, a little too calmly.

Then I began to wake up. I mean really wake up. This was about me! I also began to think that there must be some mistake. I felt fine, more or less.

"An ambulance is en route to your ship to bring you back to the Keesler Medical Facility here in Biloxi," he said. "Your blood work is consistent with liver and kidney failure. You could pass out or even die if left untreated." I was directed to get toiletries and a change of clothes, and to wait with the medics until the ambulance arrived.

I went down to my birthing to grab a few things, confident that this was some weird anomaly with my blood work and I'd be back soon after the docs figured this thing out.

A few hours later I was checked into the hospital, and the testing began immediately. There were so many blood tests over the next few weeks that my veins collapsed daily. The blood results always came in at around 3:00am and consistently indicated liver and kidney failure. But after a few more weeks of observation, urine samples, and blood analyses, the doctors decided that my liver and kidneys were functioning properly. The new concern was that my body was showing many signs of fatigue, muscular wasting, and loss of reflex response.

After a month in the hospital, my case was turned over to the neurology department. I was confused when the captain of my ship, along with my lieutenant and a few friends, came to my room with all of my belongings. My captain explained that the ship was getting underway in the next week and that I'd be temporarily assigned to Keesler A. F. B. until I could rejoin the crew. They said good-bye and wished me the best.

The medical staff spent a few weeks poking and probing my body for neurological evaluations, then decided to give me an electromyogram (EMG). An EMG measures how well the nerves can send electrical signals to the muscles. The docs needed to test my deep skeletal muscles, a process that involved sticking a four-inch needle (or electrode) into every muscle group and stimulating the muscles with electricity so the muscles contract around the electrode and give an audible reading.

The neurologist prepped me for the exam. "If we hear the sound of static or white noise, that means the muscle groups are diseased. If they make no sound, they're healthy."

The most agonizing part of the exam was that every time the doctor inserted the electrode and juiced it up, the room filled with the crackling horror of diseased muscles. About thirty minutes into the EMG I asked the doctor, "Are you sure that thing's calibrated correctly? No matter where you insert the needle, it crackles!"

He turned and said, "There's nothing wrong with the machine. Every muscle group in your body seems to be affected."

"Affected by what?" I asked nervously, noticing a glint of tears in his eyes.

"I don't know yet. We need further tests and a deep muscle biopsy, but it seems that your muscles are diseased," he explained with genuine concern.

The next week, a group of residency doctors waddled into my room behind their chain-of-command and gathered around my bed as if observing a lab rat. The callous military doctor marched over, grabbed the chart from the foot of my bed, and coldly addressed his entourage. "Here we have a twenty-year-old male – no, wait – is today your birthday?" he turned and asked me dryly.

"Yes, Sir," I replied, expecting a customary "Happy birthday" from him.

Instead he turned back to his entourage and continued, "Well, here we have a twenty-one-year-old male we suspect has either MS or MD. We are running further tests for confirmation." The solemn group then left without another word.

Now my world was really spinning. I called Mom, since she was a nurse by this time, and asked her about MS and MD. Her response was morose as she explained the prognosis for people with multiple sclerosis and muscular dystrophy. I told her not to worry and not to come to Mississippi. I would be going to San Antonio, just thirty minutes from home, for a biopsy in a week or so.

The following week I saw a neurologist who specialized in the diagnosis of neurological diseases. He took a deep muscle sample from my left hamstring, sewed me up, and sent me to the waiting room. In a few short hours the nurse took me back in. The doctor's next words would change my life forever. "You have an extremely rare form of muscular dystrophy. You need to prepare yourself for the coming changes." He then told me that the prognosis for patients with this type of MD was not good. "You will most likely be confined to a wheelchair within the next five years, but it isn't going to affect your upper extremities, so you should be alright as far as mobility."

Confined to a wheelchair?...should be alright? My mind screamed, my heart sank, and my spirit shattered. Mom cried a lot that day; Dad wasn't there. We spent the afternoon together, then Mom dropped me off at the Air Force base for my flight back to Keesler. When I stood up after the flight, the stitches in my hamstring broke and my leg started to bleed. They fixed up my leg and then checked me out of the hospital where I had spent the last two months of my life. The admin clerk informed me, "You'll be assigned a room in the barracks awaiting orders to be sent to Pensacola, Florida, for out-processing from the Navy."

"What do you mean out-processing? I still have a year and a half to go on my enlistment. Two months ago they offered to send me to college and make me an officer when I return to service!" I exclaimed, desperately trying to grasp this new reality.

HAPPY BIRTHDAY

I was informed that the military had no use for me in this condition. As far as they were concerned, I was a washout, and of no value to future military operations.

I was in complete and total shock. All of my planning and hard work to prove something to myself and to others was demolished in one day. The military was now telling me the same things Dad had told me my whole life: "You're of no value, useless, unwanted. You're damaged – a problem we need to get rid of!"

CHAPTER 3

Out-Processed

As a kid, when you're consistently told "Your life will be shit!" and "You'll never amount to anything because you're stupid!" it's hard to believe otherwise, even as an adult. These words were woven into my core belief system and a part of the same programming that Dad's father had instilled in him. As a result, there was always a glass ceiling in my life, constructed out of self-doubt and fear, that I could not seem to break through. I had given my best effort at something that was important to me, and now I felt like I had failed. I convinced myself that Dad had been right all along and was just waiting for everyone else to find out what a disappointment I was. At this point I was not aware of consciousness or the subconscious. I had no clue that I was operating my life from a subconscious state, blindly believing the negative words of others without forming my own opinions.

When I was out-processed from the Navy, I was placed under observation for five years, after which they would review my case and make a final decision on my status. The military gave me a two-hundred-dollar monthly pension for all of my trouble. All of that time and effort in the Navy had been for nothing. I had received some of the best firefighter training in the world, which was now useless. No one spoke of my accomplishments or hard work; overnight I had become nothing more than a disabled guy with a dismal future.

Lost and confused, I began to live the prognosis that the doctors had given me. I had faith in the system that raised me, and completely trusted the doctors and the military. Feeling even more fatigued and weak than before, I prepared myself for "life as a disabled veteran" and allowed muscular dystrophy to take control. A lifetime of mental and physical abuse had finally caught up to me. My mental "dis-ease" had now manifested into a physical condition – a state of disease. I was becoming more irritable and frustrated with others because I had my own problems to deal with. Entrapped in my self-rage, I lost all sympathy and concern for the plight of others.

With close friends I would occasionally try to open up and explain what had happened, but was always silenced by tears and an overwhelming sadness. It was easier to live in denial, so I rejected the emotions that were bubbling to the surface and chose to keep my inner turmoil a secret. My ego was damaged, and I was in survival mode. I put on an armor of anger and used it to keep people and emotions out of my life. I pushed away anything that reminded me of my limitations. This was my way to protect myself from further harm and from situations I was not prepared to deal with.

To make matters worse, I couldn't find a regular job because now I had a preexisting medical condition. Potential employers were not interested in my integrity, military record, or awards. All they saw was damaged goods. Many of my interviews ended with the same "We love your attitude and desire, but we just can't afford to take the risk on your future availability." This felt like another form of mental abuse. I was very hard on myself and started repeating a mantra in my head of the things Dad and others had said to me along the way: *Stupid, worthless, piece of shit. Stupid, worthless, piece of shit. Stupid, worthless…* but this only reinforced others' opinions of me and made me believe it was true.

After a few months of fruitless job searching, a friend recommended working at a nightclub. My buddy said, "Dude, you're still big and strong. Nobody'll know there's anything wrong with you if you don't tell 'em." So I lied and told them I could be a bouncer and stand up all night checking IDs. Being angry, intimidating in stature, with a hardened, empty look in my eyes that screamed "Don't jack with me!", I got the job.

After a while I was an experienced bartender at the nightclub and began fueling my weakened body with drugs and alcohol. Everyone was doing it, and the people I met in that world seemed to care more about me than anyone else. The next year and a half was a roller coaster of emotions. I was lost with no one to guide me. My life was an empty void. So I filled it with partying and working. I was miserable, but I dulled the pain by pushing the limits.

My harsh upbringing had forced me to be an independent and self-reliant person, and I thought I could take on the world. The problem was that I had no direction. Nobody was screaming in my face or telling me what to do. All my life someone had commanded me, so I never learned to be a self-starter. I was an order-taker, trying to satisfy others while ignoring my feelings and desires. My depression only got worse as it became harder to keep up physically, and everyone around me could see it. One evening at dinner with friends, a buddy of mine mentioned that the post office was hiring. "With your honorable military discharge, and being disabled, you'd get bonus points on the exam. But you know, there'll be drug testing. So maybe you should lie low on the party scene for a while."

A few months later I took the post office exam and aced the test. After training I was placed in a letter carrier position in my hometown – Hondo, of all places. They told me they liked placing people in their hometowns because the locals already "know who you are, and it's familiar." This would be a breeze, or so I thought. I ended up walking an average of twelve miles a day, six days a week. My muscular dystrophy continued to progress, and I was exhausted, but I sucked it up and plowed through, trying to pretend that it wasn't happening. Every day I had to dig deeper to find the energy just to finish the route.

My frustration was overwhelming, and my body was giving out on me. Many days I'd walk down the steps of someone's home and fall, flinging mail all over the yard. I usually lay on the ground for a moment to compose myself, then crawled around and gathered up the mail as I cursed profanely. Then I had to re-sort the mail in my bag and angrily press on.

After a year at the post office, never complaining once about my increasing fatigue, I secretly used my two-week vacation to enroll in community college. At the end of the two weeks the post office received my resignation.

The following month, my family was all together for Christmas dinner at my grandparents' house. I was proud to announce, "I quit the post office and I'm going to college!"

The news was not well received. My grandfather could not understand. "You're going to quit a good job with benefits that everybody wants? Are you crazy?"

I stood up from the table and replied, "Then everybody else can have that job, because I'm going to college!"

I was beginning to see that the only way I'd ever be truly free was by making my own choices. I wouldn't worry about what my family and friends thought of me any longer. They weren't living with muscular dystrophy, and couldn't understand. My body was stressed and breaking down at an accelerated rate. The harder I pushed, the harder it pushed back. Good or bad, this experience was mine, and I needed to forge ahead.

CHAPTER 4

Nowhere to Turn

Unlike the years back in my small-town high school, no one in college knew who I was, and neither did I. Finally, a new chapter in my life! This was a chance to reinvent myself. I was a little apprehensive about going back to school after such a long break, and four years of college seemed like a long time. All of the studying I had done up until then had been toward an immediate goal. This time I needed to commit long term and believe in myself. After three years of watching my life spiral out of control, I was finally tired of denying the effects of MD. I was ready for this new challenge, and for change. Reality was beginning to settle in, and I understood that I wouldn't be able to work in a physically demanding job. College allowed me to pursue the only other thing that interested me, which was art. I decided right away to go for a degree in graphic design. Working on the computer and being creative seemed refreshing and fun, and the perfect fit.

In order to make this new endeavor possible, I had to break up with my girlfriend of the past three-and-a-half years. This wasn't easy because she had been there for me during painfully stressful times. But the stress was starting to weigh on our relationship. We were both very young, and neither of us understood the challenges that lay ahead. Feeling as if the life I had built was falling apart, I also understood that it was time to concentrate more intently on myself for a while. In order to afford this new adventure, I had to move out of my apartment in the city and back into my old room at my parents' house. That's how much I wanted to change my life.

When I moved back home, I realized that *I* had changed, but that my parents had not. I felt the grip of control begin to tighten from the first day. Dad and the rest of my family seemed to have the attitude that I was just going to college for something to do.

They had no real expectations of my finishing school or ever doing anything with my degree... if I even got one. Dad never considered the things I was going through or the fact that I had just given up my health, independence, income, relationship, security – my entire life as I'd known it. From the beginning he had an attitude that I was just there to take advantage of him and his house for my own selfish needs.

Knowing that Dad had a volatile demeanor, I did my best to avoid an incident by working hard at school, studying long hours, working as a manager of a car wash, and coming home late. I almost never ate meals with my parents, and I pretty much kept to myself. Regardless, it didn't take long for the situation at home to deteriorate. One Sunday afternoon I came home after spending the weekend in town at my best friend Rob's apartment. The moment I walked in the door, Dad sprang out of his recliner and uncoiled his verbal assault on me. He yelled on and on about my late hours and declared that I was not coming home when he thought I should.

"I'm twenty-four years old! And I don't keep up with where you and Mom are when I come home to an empty house," I argued.

Dad shoved me and said," You don't worry about where we are because you don't give a shit about anybody but yourself!"

My response came as a surprise to Dad, and to myself. I balled up a fist and said, "Push me again and I'm gonna to knock you out!"

"Bring it, Big Boy!" he yelled, red-faced and ready to brawl.

Next thing I knew, Mom was standing between us screaming for us to calm down. I left the house for a few hours, then returned to pack my stuff and move out the next day.

It had taken only one semester of college for Dad to drive me out of the house. I moved back to the city, just down the road from Rob. I tried to look at it as a good thing; I was closer to my friends and my job, and most important to my school. This meant I'd have to work more to pay the bills, but after a successful first semester of straight As, I knew I could do it.

It didn't take long for me to get pulled back into party mode. None of my friends were in college. They all had good jobs and their nights were free to party and have fun. I thought I could just play a little bit and get my schoolwork done, too. Having a blast was what you "should" do in college. On the surface it seemed like I was handling everything with skill and grace, but on the inside I was still a mess of pain and anger. Life had somehow become a game of "Let's see how much I can get away with" – with no regard for consequences. The denial of muscular dystrophy fueled my rage. I resisted what was happening to me, always looking to push my physical limits further.

Drugs became an escape. Rob and I loved to go out riding motorcycles and racing our tuner cars in the hill country after taking several hits of acid and a couple of tabs of ecstasy. Between 2:00 and 4:00am, the roads were empty, and it felt great to escape. The exhilaration of feeling the wind, the lights flashing and racing by at high rates of speed – I had no concerns at all, and it was easy to forget about my problems. I never thought about getting hurt, and I didn't really care if I did. After punishing myself all night partying, I always wound up at the same crash site, my bed, at around 4:00am.

After a year and a half of running at full throttle, I was still maintaining a 3.8 grade point average in community college and had applied to Southwest Texas State University. My grandad got wind of my performance and asked me to come over to his house for a visit. He said he was proud of me and wanted to help pay my bills so I wouldn't have to work so hard at the University.

Someone had noticed my hard work at school! It looked like I was living the life – partying, lots of friends, nice car, cool apartment – but I was secretly full of fear and anxiety. I was so thankful that my granddad stepped up to help me out, because I was starting to run out of gas. The partying and the MD were catching up with me. My body felt exhausted all the time. This only made me angrier, which led to heightened anxiety, more drugs, and full circle to exhaustion. If my grandad had known about everything I was doing, would he still have been proud?

The University in San Marcos was about a twenty-minute drive south from Austin. At that time it was known as a party school, and I was ready and well-practiced. I signed up for twenty-one credits the first semester because I wanted to finish up and "get on with my life." With my grandad's financial help, I had the time to take on the extra hours, and I was on a mission to prove I could finish.

Community college had required a hectic commute across a city of eight million people to a flat, uninspiring downtown campus. Southwest Texas, however, was spread out along the tranquil banks of

the San Marcos River. Stately cypress trees hugged the river's edge, while huge, shady live oaks cast their cool shadows through the grassy knolls of the hilly campus. The students at Southwest were young and excited about their futures. It was a welcome change and helped me refocus on my studies for a while.

I had to start using a cane to walk around the undulating campus, as well as get a handicapped parking permit for special access. To say that these two things brought me unwanted attention is an understatement. Because of my limp and the cane, I heard frequent comments like "What are you, some kinda pimp?" The campus police constantly blocked my car in and made me show them proof that I needed the handicapped parking permit. Strangers would walk up and call me names, and lecture me for parking in a handicapped spot because "someone who looks like you can't possibly be disabled."

All of this unwanted attention made me angrier at my situation. I just wanted my life back. I just wanted to be normal. I blew it off, and never talked about what was going on with me or why I had a cane. I didn't want to burden people with my heavy story. Time raced by as I continued to party like a rock star and study feverishly to finish my degree.

In my second semester I took advanced metals class with a girl named Erin whom I had seen around the art department the previous semester. The first day of class I sat next to a friend from Louisiana and stared at Erin the entire time. About halfway through the class my buddy said to me in his lazy Southern drawl, "You're gonna sit next to her in the next class, aren't ya?"

Two days later I walked into metals class and told another friend of mine who was sitting next to Erin that he had to move over; I needed that seat. Erin and I quickly became friends. She shared her personal story with me and told me that she was a single mom. The love in her voice made it obvious to me just how proud she was of her little son.

It had been just over five years since the Navy had out-processed me and put me under observation. Soon I would have to go to Brooks Army Medical Center to finish my disability claim and have a physical. I had been dreading this appointment for a while. When I had received the diagnosis, the doctors said I had the type of muscular dystrophy that would only affect my legs and eventually force me into a wheelchair. But during the few months leading up to the appointment I had noticed that my arms felt more fatigued than usual and that my right arm looked smaller and would often go numb. I tried to ignore it, but it was beginning to worry me.

Near the end of the semester Erin noticed that I had been absent a lot, and one day she came to sit next to me outside the art building. "What's up with you? You're acting weird."

Erin, like most of my friends at school, didn't know about the MD. She knew I'd been in the Navy and probably thought my cane was from a military-related injury. So I told her the truth. "I have this thing called muscular dystrophy."

"What is that?" she asked.

I told her the whole story – about my time in the military and all about MD. Then I confessed what was really bothering me. "I have an appointment next week that I'm really nervous about. It's a medical exam. I don't think it's gonna turn out well."

Talking about all of it with Erin, I realized how alone and scared I was. Everything seemed to be catching up with me, and the high of partying all the time was starting to fade.

A week later I drove down to San Antonio for my appointment at the Medical Center. The neurologist went about his business of drawing blood, taking measurements, and strength-testing my muscle groups. I confided to him that my condition was getting worse; that it wasn't just in my legs anymore. The doctor didn't understand how I was walking in the first place, with no prosthetics and only a cane. I told him that I was stubborn and refused to use a wheelchair. He half grinned and said, "I'm really sorry, but I have some bad news. You have a more severe and aggressive type of MD than we originally thought. It looks like you're going to completely lose body control and be confined to a bed." Reduced to a pile of tears, I fought the urge to collapse onto the floor. I knew that something had been wrong, and I had tried to ignore it.

After the appointment I walked, dumbfounded, out to my black Acura Integra parked in the sizzling summer sun. I climbed into the car and just sat there in a daze. I couldn't feel the baking heat inside the car. My arms were covered in goosebumps, and all I could do was cry. The glass ceiling was now pressing against my head, crushing me, just as I was about to finish my degree. I finally realized that I was sweating profusely, so I started my car and turned on my cell phone.

When my cell picked up a signal, I saw there was a new voicemail message. Listening to the message, I heard what sounded like the voice of an angel. It was Erin. She wanted me to know that she was thinking of me and she hoped that everything had gone okay. Listening to that message over and over, my tears finally subsided, and I was able to drive back home. I never erased that message from my voicemail.

After the overwhelming news, I lost all sense of hope and my drug use began to spiral. I knew people who sold drugs and people who did drugs, and I hung out mostly with these two groups. I rarely went to class anymore. Struggling to walk around campus was just another reminder of my debilitating situation. One day some friends from the art department stopped by and said, "You should go and talk with your professors and let them know you're having a hard time right now."

I actually listened, because I was tired. I had worked hard to get to where I was and had only two semesters left to go. I felt like it was all happening so fast and I was just sitting there in school wasting away physically and watching my life pass before me. My professors were encouraging and understanding when I explained my situation, and they convinced me to stick it out. I decided to refocus, buckle down, and finish strong.

I started going to all of my classes again and turned my attention back to my degree. Erin and I had become close friends by this time, but she had a boyfriend, so it never became more than that. I had met him a few times and wasn't impressed. Erin had a two-year-old son, and her boyfriend was not the kind of guy I would hand that responsibility to.

I was in the computer lab working on a project one afternoon, and Erin walked in looking distressed. She asked me to come into the hallway. "I'm thinking about breaking up with my boyfriend," she said. "I know you've met him, so I want to know what you think."

I was jumping up and down inside. I didn't have a girlfriend, and I really liked Erin. *These things never work out, and she'll probably date somebody else*, I thought. But I agreed that she should break up with her loser boyfriend. She seemed relieved to have an answer, but apprehensive about something else.

A few nights later I had the usual party going on at my house. I was spinning records when one of my friends knocked on my headphones whispering, "I think the cops are here! Turn it down! Somebody's banging on the door!"

When I opened the door, there stood Erin in a torn t-shirt with tears streaming down her face. She looked embarrassed. "I shouldn't have come; you guys are partying... I'll go!"

I grabbed her arm. "Are you crazy? Come in! What happened?"

"My boyfriend blew up when I told him to move out. When I tried to run out, he pulled me down and tried to choke me." She sat down, took a deep breath, and said, "I got out, but panicked and didn't know where else to go. This is the only place he won't know to look!" She told me she had taken her son, Daegan, to stay with her mom, fearful that the breakup would result in a heated argument.

"Hey, it's cool if you stay here. Call your parents and wait here until they come," I said. She waited a few days for her dad to come down. We stayed up each night talking about our lives.

After she left, I waited a few months and finally built up the courage to ask her out on a date. It was a chilly November evening, and we went to a rave called Arctic II with some friends. Halfway through the night, after being friends for over a year, we finally kissed for the first time. Over the next few months Erin and I built a strong bond. We'd both been through life-changing experiences that had brought us a deeper understanding of life. As a single mom, she was dealing with things much bigger than most of the college kids around us had to deal with, and so was I. We both began to realize what the other was going through and found mutual respect and compassion for each other that went beyond a surface friendship. Erin and I started seeing more and more of each other and built a tight connection, but agreed that we should "take it slow."

One afternoon, after spending a long weekend with Erin in Austin, I came home to find an eviction notice on my door. I always gave my half of the rent to my roommate, who was supposed to pay our landlord. We'd been living together for over a year with no disagreements or problems with the rent. I called the number on the notice, and the landlord informed me that the rent had not been paid in three months. She said I had to pay it in full by Monday or the police would come and carry out the eviction. As a college student in my last semester, I had no money, at least not enough for three months of rent.

With nowhere to turn – or nowhere I'd rather turn – I drove back to Erin's apartment in Austin with the eviction notice. After filling her in on my situation she asked, "What are you going to do?"

"I honestly don't know. I thought I'd finish college this semester in my house right off campus! I don't have money to rent a new place right now!"

"I know we wanted to take it slow, but you're welcome to stay here with Daegan and me," she offered.

I moved in with Erin and got more involved in her life. I helped around the house and picked Daegan up from daycare. It was just the distraction I needed to keep me from focusing on how difficult it was becoming to do basic things like get out of the car or walk up a few steps. Time flew by, and the next thing I knew it was time for graduation.

CHAPTER 5

Lost in a Fog

After college I had a few offers to work as an intern in the graphic design industry, but I decided to take a little time off and enjoy the freedom from studies and deadlines. About a month after graduation, on the morning of September 11th, 2001, I woke up to strange sounds and reports on my alarm clock radio. Rushing to the living room, I turned on the TV just in time to see the first tower crashing to the ground. That destruction and devastation seemed to be a metaphor for my life. The potential graphic design internships crumbled into dust that day. The muscular dystrophy was getting worse. And I was battling the Department of Veterans Affairs over my disability pension and medical benefits. All of these roadblocks were beginning to take their toll on my mental health. I didn't realize it at the time, but I was slipping into a deep depression that was consuming my confidence and smothering my flame of enthusiasm.

Then a ray of sunshine entered my life when I got an internship with a film company in Austin that was filming and editing a show for HGTV. Working with creative people in a field that I was interested in gave me hope. Things seemed to be brightening up a bit, and I dreamed about future opportunities and untold experiences once again.

During this shaky period of fragile confidence, I was called in to the VA for a medical evaluation. At the evaluation I was fitted for a wheelchair and told that I needed to use it daily. I left the appointment with the wheelchair, but ignored the order and went about my life. On the outside things had never been better, but on the inside I was still a wreck. I still couldn't identify with this new reality of being disabled. After fighting and struggling, I was now being told to sit in a wheelchair and give up. At the same time part of me was tired, and maybe I was just trying to be a tough guy like I'd been raised to be.

After working a few months at the film house, I was feeling good about the future and made the best decision of my life. I asked Erin to marry me.

Erin and I had a beautiful sunset wedding and all of our friends and family were there and incredibly happy for us. The next day we boarded a plane for our honeymoon in Las Vegas. This was probably not the best choice for a person with mobility problems, and I had to take my new wheelchair. Expansive areas had to be covered to get from one casino to the next. I was not mentally ready for the stress and emotions that came flooding into my mind as a result of being trapped in a wheelchair. When my arms got tired, Erin had to push me across the thick carpets in her nice dresses and high-heeled shoes.

That first wheelchair experience left a scar on our honeymoon. We allowed the wheelchair to become the focus of our attention on that trip. I didn't know how to just "be" in the wheelchair. I needed help, and asking for the help was humiliating for me. I didn't want to burden Erin with my needs, and she didn't understand why I was so awkward and uneasy. In the end, we had fun, but wished we had gone somewhere easier where we could just relax. We were beginning to see how difficult our lives would be compared to most people our age. It was frustrating, to say the least, and my resistance and frustration only built up from there.

Back from the honeymoon, we headed back to reality. Erin had just started a career in the video game industry and I was trying to figure out whether or not to pursue TV and film. Living in a small two-bedroom apartment, we were busting at the seams, so we began searching for a home. I drove around with the broker, and Erin and I talked endlessly about real estate. After buying a beautiful four-bedroom American dream, I got my real estate license and worked for the broker who sold us our house. I liked the energy and ideas the broker had, and I enjoyed his company and guidance. He was like a father figure to me, and someone I could learn a lot from.

He was the first person to introduce me to the ideas of goal-setting and self-improvement. Patient and compassionate, he had two attributes that I was short on but admired. We spent hours talking about quality of life and how to improve it, but I had a hard time understanding how to put it all into action. My frame of mind was stuck in fear and anger, and after watching Dad stress about his lack of money my whole life, I couldn't shift from dreading scarcity to seeing the abundance that was all around me. I started to believe another lie: that my life was not abundant. Sure, we had a nice house, two nice cars, and good jobs, but I thought I was supposed to have more. I believed that abundance and quality of life meant lots of money.

I eventually left my mentor and moved on to another real estate office, seeking a more lucrative commission in an upscale market. I had the best idea: I'd take the principles and concepts I'd learned from my first broker and expand on them until I was overwhelmed with success and money.

The new broker liked my attitude and concepts on quality of life, abundance, and customer care so much that I was asked to write a training program. Before I knew it I was the new agent trainer at the brokerage. I was teaching other agents a system that worked and produced results, but the same concepts I was teaching weren't working for me. The problem was that I understood the concepts on an intellectual level, but I was not in harmony with my desires on a conscious or subconscious level. I was allowing the scarcity mentality from my financially strained childhood to once again hold me back.

The more I watched others succeed financially, the more self-loathing I became. Bitter and resentful, I believed that if I didn't have this physical handicap I would be the top agent in any office. Trapped in a cycle of blame and misunderstanding, I became a victim of my own mind. Externalizing all of my problems, I convinced myself that I was smart and knew the secrets to "success," but that my physical challenge was holding me back.

My mind was in one place and my spirit and physical body were trapped in reality. I had left my first broker in search of higher success; instead I was teaching others how to achieve their dreams while mine sat stagnant and lifeless in the corners of my mind. In harmony with negativity at the time, I couldn't understand or accept that my perspective and projections were the causes of my failures. I was so successful at personal failure that I cut all spiritual and physical ties to my body and lived only in my head, repeatedly attempting to figure it all out and always coming up empty. Unable to find the answers, I became ensnared in the same feelings of rage and bitterness I had experienced as a child.

These negative thought patterns created stress that started to affect my body in a more pronounced way. The back and joint pain that I had rarely felt before became so severe that my doctors sent me to get MRIs and CAT scans to see if there was physical damage. The findings were always inconclusive. In other words, there was no physical cause for my pain. Destructive thought patterns and a poor mental state were causing my physical pain, but the doctors at the VA focused only on the pain. With no physical ailment to treat, their only apparent option was to prescribe hydrocodone and muscle relaxers. Since I'm a big guy, they gave me the maximum dosage of both and told me to stay away from other drugs and alcohol. So of course I went home, washed down a few pills with some beer, and passed out.

My new routine: pop some pills and throw a little alcohol into the mix while cooking dinner. The cycle became so addictive that I eventually moved my office to my home. I like to think that I moved to a home office so I could be more productive and have more time with my son; in reality it was easier to take calls and answer real-estate questions while I was pilled-out in the comfort of my home.

I rapidly started to lose touch with reality and stopped caring about myself. As I slipped deeper into depression, Erin realized something was wrong

and tried to help. "I think you're depressed. Maybe you should try talking with someone."

I responded in anger. "I'm fine! I don't need anyone's help!"

Each day she would leave for work and I would overeat, take a handful of hydrocodone, and run Daegan to and from school.

This went on for a year or so, until one day I realized that I had forgotten to pick up Daegan at school and I freaked out. Jumping out of my office chair, I frantically grabbed the keys and had barely opened the garage door when I heard footsteps behind me. Daegan came walking down the hall and said in his little five-year-old voice, "Where are you going, Daddy?"

Now I was really struggling to get a grip on the situation. "How did you get home?" I asked, puzzled.

"You picked me up, remember?" he said, smiling as if it was a joke.

But I couldn't remember! I tried and tried, but my head was so foggy that I couldn't find the memory of leaving, driving, or returning home with my son. It was this day that I realized I had an addiction and that it had become a major problem. But I was confused. I was taking the doses the doctor prescribed me, right? Furthermore, how could I deal with the pain without the meds?

I didn't have the answers but I knew it had to stop. It was not just about me anymore, and I didn't want anything bad to happen to my family because of my addiction to pills. It scared me so badly that I told Erin, and she helped convince me that I didn't need the meds. "You're always in pain anyway, even when you take them. They're only covering up the problem and causing new ones."

I finally realized that the drugs were only dulling my senses and poisoning my mind and body. It's hard to overcome an addiction, especially when you're using it to avoid pain. At my next exam the VA doctors asked why I had stopped refilling my pain meds. When I told them about my dependency problems, they argued with my decision and informed me, "Your dependency on the pills is because your body needs them."

CHAPTER 6

Adjustment Disorder

It wasn't easy to quit, but I did it. The first battle I had to face was with myself. It was mentally and physically painful to taper off the addiction. Every day seemed more difficult than the last because the pain was no longer dulled to the point that I was only subconsciously aware of it.

After a few months of struggle I was completely off the pills, and my VA doctor called me in for a consult. Once seated, my doctor of seven years said to me, "I need you to do a few things for me today. If you can't do the exercises, the VA has decided that you must be in a wheelchair at all times. You will not be allowed to walk into the VA with your cane, and instead you must report to all appointments in your wheelchair."

The Texas tough guy came bubbling to the surface, and I declared, "You can't make me use the wheelchair. It's my choice and I don't think I need it."

"Okay, then, get down on the floor and get up without your cane or a chair to aid you," he said, knowing full-well that wasn't possible. He then instructed me to complete several other exercises that he knew I couldn't perform.

Baffled, I finally had to ask, "What exactly are you trying to prove here?"

"I'm gauging your ability to walk, and noting that in my opinion you don't have the muscular strength needed," he stated bluntly.

"I've been walking into this office for the last seven years and nothing ever happened. And I'll just keep walking in."

He put up his hand to stop me and firmly warned, "No, you won't. If you can't do these exercises, you are leaving here today in a wheelchair."

Standing up, I felt the need to defend myself. "If you threaten me, or ask me to do one more thing that you know I can't do, I'm gonna show you what I can do – which is put my fist through your face!" I was really letting it all out now. "All you can see is what's on the outside. But inside my chest beats the heart of a warrior, and I won't let you or anybody else tell me what I can and can't do!"

His face turned pale as he ran for the door. I sat waiting like the dutiful patient. When the door opened, two large security officers appeared and told me to get up and come with them. My doctor had no problem with my walking out of his office and down a half-mile of hallways to the mental health center. They called me in for a psychological evaluation, which put me in a rage. I asked the first psychiatrist, "So this is how it happens? I stand up for myself, show concern about my health situation, and now I'm the troublemaker? Why, because I refused pain meds and said I don't want to sit in a wheelchair? Isn't this my life and my choice?"

He informed me that I was being difficult and suffering from a type of severe "adjustment disorder." Within five minutes he concluded that I should be on powerful antianxiety and antidepressant medications.

Having just cleaned myself up from the last pills prescribed by the VA, I was vehemently opposed. "As far as I know, those pills aren't going to change the situation or make my physical health any better.

So keep 'em... I'm not interested! You have no idea what I'm going through. I didn't ask to be here and I didn't ask for your opinion!"

Agitated and uncomfortable, the therapist gave up. "You think you're so smart; I'm going to get another therapist to talk some sense into you."

The next guy attempted to tell me more of the same. "You need to be medicated. You're depressed." But he could see that I was in no mood to hear it. He lasted about five minutes before saying that he couldn't handle my attitude, and then he passed me off to the director of psychology.

The first thing I noticed when speaking with the director was that she was not accustomed to being questioned. I asked her how they could make a diagnosis within five minutes of talking to a new patient without knowing anything about his background or medical history or asking any personal questions.

Her attitude shifted, and she retorted, "Here's some personal history questions: Are you married? Do you have kids? Do you use illegal drugs like marijuana?"

I became quiet as I saw what was happening. After collecting my thoughts, I replied, "I know

what you're doing. You want to discredit and judge me because surely anyone using marijuana or any other drug is irrational, right? All you want to do is make me feel bad – as if I can't handle my problems. And then medicate me to "fix" them. How does your position make more sense than mine? At least I know what's going on in my life and what mental state or mood I'm in. I came here today for a checkup. And just because I said I don't want to use a wheelchair, I'm now being held against my will, having drugs pushed on me without my consent, and being questioned about my personal life."

Her only response was, "Well, you can tell us about your drug abuse or not, but you're not leaving here without a drug test."

I could see that I was dealing with emotionless robots, so I just started naming off one drug after another, listing everything that I had ever done. I didn't care anymore; I just wanted to get the hell out of there. When I finished I said, "Are you happy now? You and your colleagues can slap each other on the back and say 'I told you so – he's on drugs!'"

The director was not impressed. "Do you know what your real problem is? You think you're so smart, but we got you."

"Well I must be smarter than you because I answered your question honestly in spite of your threats and coercion. It must really bother you that I have the answers to all of your questions and yet you can't answer even one of mine!" I looked her hard in the eyes and finished by saying, "All that I keep doing is asking logical questions that you and your colleagues ignore, deflect, and undermine in an effort to push pills and quiet my voice. You're not helping anybody here; you're just throwing pills at problems."

She was really pissed off now, and escorted me to another office where she walked away mumbling to herself, "I can't deal with this!"

A few minutes later the fourth therapist of the day came walking into the tiny little closet of an office and introduced himself as David. I immediately noticed that there were two large prescription bottles on his desk with my name on them. I jumped back exclaiming, "I already told the other therapists I'm not taking any more pills."

David said respectfully, "I can see that you're upset. You calm down and I'll be back in a few minutes."

ADJUSTMENT DISORDER

After a few minutes alone I felt more at ease. David returned, relaxed into the chair across from me, and asked, "Why are you here today?"

Now, that was a great place to start! I summarized the whole story, starting with the checkup that day, then moving backward in time to getting tossed out of the military like a piece of trash "because I was damaged, and they were done with me. I was never offered any type of support or counseling on how to deal with my issues or my anxiety about my health and my future. Now today, because I don't want to use a wheelchair and their drugs, I'm a head case and need counseling! Where was all this help in the beginning when I was lost and confused? Oh, that's right, nobody gave a shit. But now that I want to make my own choices and take care of myself, I'm the crazy troublemaker who can't deal with his problems and needs to be medicated?"

After talking for a while, I noticed how patiently David was listening while jotting in his notepad, and that he seemed to understand. I liked him, and felt comfortable asking him a few questions. He told me he was from Colorado and had just graduated from the University of Texas with a degree in psychology. I asked him a few more personal questions and he responded as if talking to a friend. After a short back and forth, David set down his pen, looked up at me, and said, "You're really good at what you do, and you don't even know it."

"What do you mean I'm really good at what I do? What am I doing?" I asked.

"I'm sitting here telling you all about my life and feeling really good about myself, but I'm supposed to be the one counseling you. You seem to understand things about people on an intuitive or subconscious level, and then you quickly give them what they need to feel comfortable so they open up to you. This is a skill that many people in my profession work years to try and master, yet you've perfected it and don't even realize it. Furthermore, you don't even recognize that it's a skill and that you have a gift."

David explained that kids with difficult childhoods often develop coping skills that help calm situations and redirect the attention to something besides themselves. "I'm not certain, but I'm pretty sure that as we dive deeper into your past, we'll discover that you were the protector and the negotiator in your family. We may find that you have been aligning yourself with the thoughts and ideas of others in order to feel recognized and yet keep the focus away from yourself."

Then he wanted to talk more about living with muscular dystrophy and what I'd been through. I wanted him to see my perspective – why I was depressed yet refusing the pills – so I asked, "What would you do and how would you feel if we could trade places and you could see and feel what it's like to have your life taken from you? What if something that you never wanted or asked for was grinding down your body and shattering your soul?" David waited quietly for me to continue. "If you were me and trying to sort all this out, wouldn't you want to have mental awareness, thoughts, and emotions, all of which we use to cope with difficult changes in our lives? Maybe I'm wrong and I shouldn't be so pissed off. Maybe I'm sad and I shouldn't be so irritable. But maybe I need to be sad and pissed off today so that I can feel glad and laugh about something tomorrow, you know? I'm not always angry. Y'all are just seeing me today in this moment of extreme anxiety and frustration. But I do know these feelings need to be felt and sorted out. Those pills on your desk aren't going to help me. They'll only dull my depression and pacify the pain." I finished, and looked up at David.

He returned a peaceful gaze and said, "I believe you are one of the sanest people that I've ever spoken

with, and I agree that you need to sort your feelings and deal with them in a natural way. I can also see that you're severely depressed, and rightfully so. I don't want you to take these meds either, but *they* do, so you have to sign this document saying that you will take these meds and report every Friday afternoon to mandatory psychological evaluations and rehabilitation." The anger must have shown on my face, because David told me to calm down and listen. "If you don't sign this, you're not leaving here today. Then you won't have the choice of taking meds or not. Do you understand?" He then told me not to take the pills, but instead to dump the bottles and refill them every month.

After signing the paper, I grabbed the pills and then grudgingly remembered to ask, "Oh yeah, where do I go for the drug test so that I can go home?"

"What drug test? We can't drug test you. You're not active duty military and you're not under suspicion of anything," he replied.

From one of the most frustrating, darkest experiences I can remember, an opportunity emerged that day that changed my life – a chance to express my feelings to an unattached person who just listened with no criticism.

Weeks flew by as David and I dove into the depths of my abusive, misunderstood childhood. Together we unearthed answers to decisions and behaviors I had previously not understood. We found common ground and he could relate to me. We were both young men, recently married, with a small child at home. Discussions were usually about family life, both past and present, and my perspective on being a father as opposed to being a son.

David asked me how I handled situations that arose at home with my wife and son. Then we compared them to the way things had been dealt with in my parents' home. The differences in the two households showed me that I was stopping the pattern and making my own path. Realizing that I had more control over my life than I had thought, I started shifting away from the reactionary anger I had witnessed and felt.

For the first time I was beginning to see myself, and my disability, in a different light. I could see that I had always felt like the victim of my circumstances, which made me feel shame for my choices. Due to this way of thinking, I had placed my recovery and well-being in the hands of a system that saw me as a number. I had become convinced that someone, or some pill, would be the cure for all my problems.

David helped me understand that many of the solutions I was looking for could be discovered through inner reflection. Through meditation I could have an effect on my outer world by exploring my inner world. He guided me to the "director's chair" of my mind. I realized that I had been an actor reacting to other roles and situations being played out in my reality; but as the director I could change the script, decide to take action, and control my reactions to others.

This one small piece of advice, offered by my therapist, began my process of personal transformation. I was beginning to see from a new perspective, which allowed me to create new opportunities. By becoming the director, I gained insight into the stories that had been playing out in my mind. What a revealing but difficult seat to be in! Most of the stories I had starred in were sad and depressing, with me as the victim and perpetrator. All I needed to do now was develop a new storyline and sculpt this character into an award-winning star!

CHAPTER 7

Shoving Off

After a year of counseling, I was finally starting to take back my direction and purpose. I felt ready for a big endeavor that would shatter the old story and help me restructure my life and my new role. Although the weekly therapy sessions were the reason for my confidence, they were full of negative memories that I was tired of rehashing over and over again. Something was pushing me on to the next thing, making me feel uncomfortable in my current environment. I finally said to Erin, "I don't know why, but I don't feel like I belong here anymore!" She had also grown tired of the rat race that our life had become and wanted to make a change.

At first we thought about moving somewhere else in the States, but then a friend suggested we visit Costa Rica. He thought it might be a good fit and just the change of pace we were looking for. So we took our first family vacation to Costa Rica, and liked it so much that it was hard to return home. The people there were friendly, it was peaceful, and everything was bursting with color and life. Erin and I agreed that we'd love to move there, but took no steps to make it happen, and dreamed about it for a year.

The dream seemed so possible and real at first. But over time it began to fade. At Christmastime, realizing that we were slipping back into a hectic, materialistic lifestyle, we started having serious conversations again about moving to Costa Rica. We discussed how difficult it would be, how our friends and families would feel, and that Erin's dream job in the video game industry, which had taken dedication and extreme effort to achieve, would have to be abandoned. We had a nice home that we had invested money, time, and love into. It was filled with electronics, furniture, two new cars, and Erin's grand piano, all of which we'd have to sell. But I was sure that there was a life beyond these possessions, and was ready for adventure and discovery. We tackled one problem at a time and formed a plan to leave it all behind and live out our dream.

When I announced that we were leaving, most people thought I had lost my mind. Our friends and family were not as excited as we were. When I told Mom that I was going to sell everything and move to Costa Rica with my wife and son, she looked at me as if to say, "Oh Jeff, you're such a dreamer!" She brushed it off as a desire to run away, and didn't seem to believe it would happen. It was hard to explain my reasons for leaving because I didn't understand them completely myself. My instinct was telling me to go, and I was finally listening to it.

I allowed everyone to have their opinions, and moved on with the plan to get out of debt, save money, and sell everything. This was a tough exercise in personal growth and letting go. Many times I stopped and questioned myself: "What am I doing?" "How will we get rid of all this stuff?" "How can we make all of this happen?" Every time I asked a question, an answer was given as if something was guiding me, almost pushing me, out the door. Our house was featured on the cover of a high-profile real estate magazine, which landed us a contract soon afterward. Erin found someone

at work looking for a Honda S2000, and they purchased her car without our having to place an ad. Dad surprisingly offered to buy my truck and let me use it until we moved. That only left one last, big challenge: selling Erin's grand piano. I called a piano tuner to get it cleaned and tuned up, and he found us a buyer within the week.

When everything had been sold and the house was mostly empty, we had a going away party with our close friends. It was surreal; such a mix of emotions. I heard everything from "Are you crazy? Your life is awesome here in Austin! You have everything!" to "I get why you're doing it. I wish I had the guts to drop everything and move." It was refreshing to look around the house and feel free of all the possessions. I finally understood that we had worked so hard to buy things only to worry about those things and later replace what we had been worried about with new, more expensive things. It was all external, and external things can never bring lasting joy.

Adventure was on the horizon, but I had one last challenge to face before we went – Dad. It was our last day in Austin and my parents were coming to pick up the truck and have a farewell lunch with us. I picked a local Cajun place, knowing that Dad loves

SHOVING OFF

Cajun food. As soon as they showed up at the house, I could tell this wouldn't be a joyous send-off. It was apparent that Mom was upset. My dream of moving to Costa Rica was now a reality.

After a few awkward minutes in the empty house, I suggested that we drive over to the restaurant. I thought, *It'll be cool to ride with Dad in the truck he's buying from me.* Everyone else rode in a separate car. During the ride to the restaurant, Dad was painfully quiet. I could tell that he was agitated, but that was nothing out of the ordinary for him.

We arrived and sat down at a large round table to enjoy a last meal with my family before leaving. Just as our drinks arrived, Dad exploded, "So when you move, are you gonna write or reply to emails? Or are you just gonna ignore 'em like you do now!"

I looked at Dad and tried to explain honestly, "Sending someone a forward or a bunch of spam isn't writing someone an email; it's spamming. And no one I know responds to spam."

He was getting red in the face, so I quickly added, "If you have something you want to say, then write me an email and I'll gladly write you back."

Erupting from his chair, Dad stood up from the table and spewed, "I guess you got what you wanted from me. I bought that truck of yours, so now you can move!"

I know that somewhere behind the outburst he was really just upset that we were leaving. But I was tired of taking it and allowing myself to be a victim. "If that's what you think, then I can't change your mind. Why are you so mad anyway? You never write emails; you just send forwards and jokes. Am I supposed to respond to every spam email I get? Like I already said, if you write me a personal email, I'll write you back."

Shoving away from the table, he gave his brand of a fatherly farewell. "Good luck in Costa Rica, asshole. Don't bother to call or email 'cause I don't give a shit!"

Storming off, he climbed into my old truck and drove away. We choked down lunch while my aunt talked about how rude Dad was. On the way home Mom said, "I know why you're moving to Costa Rica, and if you think you're going to escape all your problems, you're wrong! You may be upset with your Dad right now, but you owe him an email or two every now and then."

SHOVING OFF

When we arrived at the house, Dad was sitting in the truck, parked on the street. Mom and my aunt hugged us good-bye, and everyone left. Dad never rolled down his window to say good-bye, not even to his grandson.

The next morning, we pulled away from our house for the last time, pausing in the driveway to cry (all three of us) and release a whirlwind of emotions.

We got to the hotel in Houston and met up with our friend Kevin who was helping us move. Finally, some sanity and easy friendship amid the chaos! Kevin helped us get refocused and excited about the journey ahead. And what a challenge we had created for ourselves. We didn't exactly have a rental house in Costa Rica or any plans other than "a friend of a friend" named Alvaro who would pick us up at the airport and let us use his cabin until we sorted things out. It was all in the hands of fate now.

CHAPTER 8

Cold Shower

We came rolling into the Costa Rican airport like a low-budget circus, with three dogs, three adults, a seven-year-old, and two cat kennels full of pee. Daegan pushed my wheelchair through the crowd, weaving left and right like a drunken monkey while I held tight to the tower of animals and bags piled in my lap. Erin and Kevin maneuvered wobbly carts overloaded with luggage and soiled dog kennels. The pungent animal odor made us high-priority passengers, and like international dignitaries we were rushed through customs with no delay.

I'm so thankful that Kevin was there to ease the transition and lighten the mood. Sitting outside the

airport waiting for a ride to who knew where, Kevin played the guitar and we laughed about the insanity of the situation. Kevin was feeling many of the same emotions that we were at that time in his life. He had just quit his job and was struggling with the idea of telling his overly conservative parents that he had a boyfriend. We were all stepping into the great unknown together, which felt scary and exhilarating at the same time.

Alvaro, the friend-of-a-friend we were expecting, soon pulled up in a large SUV and jumped out to greet us. He had cheerful, smoky brown eyes and welcomed us as if we were old family friends, with hugs, kisses, and handshakes all around. He carefully loaded our stinky cargo, insisting that everything was *"solo bueno"* (or "all good") when we apologized for the mess. We were blasted by the beauty of the Costa Rican cloud forest as we left the capital city of San Jose and wound through the mountains. Alvaro drove us to a little mountain town called Turrialba and up to the cabin that we were renting for the next few weeks.

In Austin we had wished to be free of possessions and simplify our lives, and apparently that wish was being fulfilled. Expecting a cozy cabin atop the mountain equipped with a fireplace, thick rugs, and cozy beds, we were shocked to walk into an uninsulated, barren room. The small bedroom off to the side had a bunk bed and a twin bed for the four of us to share. No appliances, anywhere. When Alvaro mentioned that the electricity wouldn't be hooked up for at least a week, we added candles to the grocery list. He introduced us to our next door neighbors who had a wood-burning stove and a washboard. He said they could cook meals for us and do our laundry for a small fee. I quickly realized that I should have learned Spanish before I came.

After a week of cold showers and eating out of an ice chest, we took our first road trip to the Caribbean town of Puerto Viejo for Erin's birthday. Kevin and I had both brought gifts with us from the States and had wrapped them in banana leaves and tropical flowers. Kevin's gift was a DVD called *The Secret*, which was about manifesting your dreams. "I loved that movie! It's exactly how we got here!" I told him. "We're realizing our dreams right now by being in Costa Rica!" Kevin gave us an extra, unexpected gift that night: confirmation that the power of intention works.

I asked Kevin about his dreams. "If you could have any job, what would it be?"

"I've always wanted to make robots or kids' interactive toys. I'd also like to get back into my painting and art," he confessed.

"Kevin, if we could pull this off, then anything is possible. Make that your heart's desire and go for it!" I encouraged him.

The next week, back at the cabin, Kevin played his guitar late into the night while Erin and I formed a plan for where to live. Our neighbors were at our cabin every day helping us learn Spanish, which was starting to make life easier. We had a long road ahead, and so much to figure out, but we tried to stay focused on the immediate concerns.

It came time for Kevin to fly back home. He was the last tie to our old life, and we were about to be all alone on this adventure. We dropped him off at the airport and expressed how thankful we were for his help and support during the move.

The next few weeks felt a little sad and lonely as we rushed to appointments with customs agents and lawyers, applied for residency, looked for a school, and searched for a house. Everything required us to learn more Spanish, and it was happening at a much faster rate than I had expected. Needing to learn Spanish was a blessing in disguise because it gave us something to focus our attention on when things weren't going well, which seemed to be often at first. There were times in those first few weeks when I questioned our decision. We were all alone in a new country, didn't speak the language, and every mistake was costly. I just forced myself to believe that it would all work out as long as we kept faith and wanted to be there.

Forging ahead, we found a nice private school in San Jose for Daegan and started looking at houses in the area. But while driving to the school to turn in the paperwork, we got stuck in rush-hour traffic! Honking horns and the smell of exhaust – it felt like we were back in Austin! We realized we were making a mistake, and made a U-turn on the spot. It was time to come up with plan B.

After wrapping up the last of our stressful business in the city, we decided to head over to the Pacific coast for my birthday. Driving down the jungle-lined coastal highway, the salty air filling our lungs, Erin and I couldn't stop grinning at each other. I could feel the excitement and sense that this was what we had been longing for. We drove deep into the jungle, just off the beach, to a tiny village called Ojochal.

Ojochal is a quaint little town of about four hundred people less than a kilometer from the beach. It's a place where nature has expressed its majesty with lush, green mountains that give birth to cascading waterfalls and wild, winding rivers that open their mouths to kiss the sea. It was 2006, but there were no telephones or internet service, and nature was reluctant to give way to the technology of man.

The only forms of communication in the village were two-way radios and word of mouth. I'm still not sure which was faster. The dirt roads were dusty and bumpy in the dry season and slippery mud pits in the rainy season. Only a grocery store, hair salon, and two open-air restaurants lined the potholed road. It was a forty-minute drive to the nearest bank or hospital and a four-hour drive to the nearest mall. It made me think of a small U.S. town back in the '50s where everyone knew who was who and what was what. What it lacked in conveniences it more than made up for in quality of life. Ojochal was just the kind of environment we wanted after leaving our hectic lives in the States. Before we left that week, we put down a deposit on a rental house up in the mountains overlooking the rainforest.

COLD SHOWER

Back in Turrialba, we packed and prepared for the move to Ojochal. Our Spanish had improved thanks to being secluded on a mountaintop with our Spanish-speaking neighbors, and we were thrilled to continue our adventure. We'd be in the new house before Daegan's eighth birthday, with Christmas soon to follow.

CHAPTER 9

Are You Happy?

Growing up in Texas, I saw plenty of insects, snakes, and other unwelcome vermin, but nothing like the hand-sized spiders and armored centipedes that inhabited our first rental house in Ojochal. When we drove up just two weeks after paying the deposit, it was already overgrown with jungle and crawling with oversized insects. But it wasn't anything a hefty can of bug spray couldn't handle.

The jungle house soon showed other faults. During the first tropical storm it was transformed into a jungle swamp filled with three inches of water. We easily decided it was time to move, and rented a place farther up the mountain – still no telephone,

TV, or internet, but a comfortable, well-built home where we could stay dry.

All of the seemingly insurmountable problems that I'd solved so far were making it easier to take on bigger challenges. I spent a few months learning the area and meeting people, then decided to invest in a lush river property down in the village. It included an old house and a guest cabin that both needed some work – my first real project in Costa Rica! It would be easy to turn that property around. I'd manage the construction and buy materials, and hire someone to do the work. We had been there six months, my Spanish was improving, and I was confident in my decisions.

A friend introduced me to a builder named Andrey, better known as "Rasta," and construction began right away. Rasta was an arduous worker and quickly became a family friend. But even beyond that, he had a giant smile and an easy stride that drew me in. Rasta loved the ocean, and every afternoon after work we stopped to have a beer and watch the sun set over the sea. He lived along the bountiful banks of the largest river in Costa Rica, and told me wild stories about surfing and swimming in the croc-infested river mouth. Listening to his stories, discussing construction, and making daily trips to the hardware store improved my Spanish exponentially. Rasta often expressed gratitude for the things he was learning while working with me, but I felt my life was equally enriched from working side by side with one of the most patient, kindest men I'd ever known.

The only problem was that the more progress we made on the house, the more debt Erin and I acquired. Just when we were starting to run dangerously low on funds, we were asked to run a hotel for two months. We lived at the hotel, which saved us rent money, and were paid a fee by the owners. This gave us a little breathing room financially, but it didn't take long to get sucked back into the rat race, running around solving other people's problems. I had to be in the kitchen by 4:30am to cook breakfast each day, after which I'd rush down on my ATV to check on the house construction, give the crew instructions, and buy materials. If there was a problem or question, I'd have to solve it quickly and then rush back to the hotel to cook dinner. We weren't allowed to leave the hotel unattended, so Erin and I had to take turns running errands. We couldn't even go down to the property together to discuss the construction.

Just before the owners of the hotel returned, a friend asked us to house-sit their new home while they went to Canada for a month. This would save us another month of rent that we could put back into the house, so we agreed to help them out.

One night, two weeks after leaving the hotel, we were in the bathroom getting ready for bed when Erin walked up and said, "Jeff, there's something I have to tell you. The way I feel right now – I've only felt this way one other time in my life." While I took a minute to piece together this cryptic information, her smile grew bigger with anticipation. She finally burst out, "The last time I felt this way, I was pregnant!"

I broke into hysterical laughter, and Erin asked, "Why are you laughing like that? Are you happy?"

Still laughing, I said, "I just checked our bank account today, and we're down to thirty-five dollars!" What else could I do but laugh? This was the happiest accident of my life. I did wonder how we would squeeze a new baby into our tight budget, but I had learned that it's amazing what you can accomplish when you have no other choice.

The opportunity to look after the house we were living in made me think of other new houses being built and that these absentee owners would need a property manager. I could hire Rasta to be a dependable, highly capable right-hand man for the business, taking care of all the things I was physically incapable of doing. With my combination of real estate, firefighting, and maintenance experience, I felt like property management would be a good fit and provide the extra money we would need. Now I just needed to structure and monetize the idea. I worked out a plan, spoke with potential clients, and within two weeks I had two houses to manage! The business took off immediately, and I had endless requests for overdue maintenance and small construction projects.

One morning I picked up Rasta as usual and noticed the almond trees outside of his house were full of scarlet macaws. There had to be twenty or thirty of them squawking and chattering away as they devoured the bounty of almonds. I parked my ATV under the tree and the birds started bombing me with their litter.

Rasta came out laughing. "You should move before they start dropping other stuff on you!"

"Dude, you have no idea how cool this is! They can drop whatever they want on me!" I exclaimed. We sat there for the better part of an hour just watching the feeding frenzy.

When our attention was focused on the job at hand, Rasta was the hardest worker I'd ever known. He could carry out the work of two men and yet moved with smooth grace in the stifling tropical heat. I marveled at the amount of work this happy, humble man could accomplish. Rasta seemed to harvest joy from everything he did. The more difficult the job, the farther that giant smile of his stretched across his face. His smile kept me in check when things got frustrating and I wanted to fly off the handle. He showed me patience and humility in the face of overwhelming circumstances.

Rasta and I were blazing through the jungle to check on a property when he spotted something and said, "Slow down! Slow down!" I reluctantly pulled over, feeling rushed to stay on schedule.

"What? What's up?" I asked.

"Let's check out that old abandoned house over there." He pointed out the remains of a small farmhouse nestled under a cluster of enormous mango trees. It had an amazing view of the ocean.

I drove the ATV through the thick overgrowth for a closer look. "I thought you'd think this was cool," Rasta said. "This house is ancient, Man, from before

anybody else lived here. No roads. No electricity. Before this was even Ojochal."

These "poor" people had nothing by society's modern standards. Yet from another perspective they had it all – a comfortable seaside home built out of exotic hardwoods with an amazing view of the ocean. "After all these years, I can't believe it's still standing. Obviously it wasn't hard to find nice hardwoods back then. Check it out, we're surrounded by 'em!" I laughed and thought how ironic it was that I had just spent a fortune on wood for my house.

"Yeah, Man, they had it all. Look at all the mango trees and bananas. It's the perfect spot. No bugs, cooler at night." He motioned to the clear, spring-fed river lined with fruit trees. "As much fresh water as they needed."

"You can see over there, where they had a farm," I said, nodding towards the old wooden fence posts that had grown roots and turned back into trees. "Free-range pigs and chickens. Organic eggs, fruits, and vegetables provided daily."

"And you know how it is here... people are all about hunting. They would've had traps and tons of

animals to eat," he added. "Everything they needed was right here. They probably felt rich!"

It reminded me of an old pioneer homestead back in the States; settlers living off the land. Rasta had made me slow down and open my eyes to this seemingly meaningless little scene. These people weren't deprived; they had lived in abundance. They knew that everything they needed was right in front of them and lived in harmony with nature. This was what quality of life was all about – true wealth and happiness. I couldn't imagine being more present than that family who truly and completely lived in the moment. I had spent the majority of my life around successful, educated people who had never grasped this concept. Ironically it was my "uneducated" friend from Costa Rica who hadn't finished the sixth grade who taught me this lesson.

CHAPTER 10

Shattered

The rainy season in the Southern Pacific zone of Costa Rica starts in May and ends as the year closes in December. This is the time of the heaviest rainfall of the year, when plants and animals regenerate and bathe in the abundant showers. It's also when the old is replenished by the new – the rainforest's version of winter. Many of the old forest trees, with their aged and weakened roots, fall and give way to eager saplings racing to meet the sun.

My property management business was soaring, the house construction was progressing, and our son, Kai, was born. In order to save money, we moved into the house that Rasta and I had been tirelessly working on. It wasn't finished, but by not paying rent we were able to put more money into the house. I was feeling pretty good about my decisions and settling into life in Costa Rica. However, I was so focused on work and making money that I was neglecting myself.

It was increasingly hard to get around. My weight issue was out of control, and even rolling over in the bed was difficult and frustrating. The muscular dystrophy that I had been working so hard to deny was always looming in the corner. I was depressed, weak, fat, and angry. All of my efforts to reject what was happening to me had backfired. My denial and self-loathing had only accelerated the process of degradation in my body. It was like I was punishing myself for carrying so much pain. I had a beautiful wife, two amazing sons, was living in Costa Rica by the beach, and still hated my life. What the hell was the matter with me? I was stuck in a self-destructive mode, and nothing could convince me to change.

With all this angst poisoning my mind, weakening my spirit, and ravishing my body, I started to fall more frequently. Every time I found myself on the floor I would think, *Wow, that hurt, and now I can't get up without some help. I really need to listen to Erin and start losing some weight.* Of course after I was back on my feet and the minor pain of whatever injury I had sustained had passed, I didn't think further about losing weight or getting serious about my situation. So I just stayed miserable and stuck.

Mom came down to celebrate Kai's first birthday. We all went to a mountain town in the cloud forest called Monteverde. It's a beautiful town, but the trip was difficult for me due to limited access. I had to miss out on the hiking, zip lines, and ATV tours, and just watch from the sidelines. Being overweight had further impaired my mobility. The frequency of my falls had increased. I used to fall down about once a year, but lately I'd been falling once a month. Instead of recognizing my faults, I blamed the outside world for my problems, feeling helpless about my situation. Erin was frustrated with my anger and lack of patience. But the more frustrated she got, the more impatient I became. I was stuck, once again, in a cycle of self-inflicted pain. But I tried to suck it up and enjoy the week with my mom.

A few more months went by, and I continued to eat too much and exercise my negative state of mind. I was stuck in a deep hole, and all I could do was keep digging. It got to the point that the only voice I could hear was my own. The positive support Erin tried to offer didn't matter to me anymore; I was lost in my own mental hell. Anxiety and depression had burned my self-esteem to the ground. I was fully ablaze, with anger and regret fueling my self-destructive tendencies.

After a long Saturday, after everyone went to sleep, I got up to lock the doors, turn off the lights, and check on the kids. I flipped off the kitchen light and headed down the hall, holding on to the wall for support. My foot landed on something hard and slipped out from under me, throwing me off balance. Like a tree whose roots had lost their support, I crashed forwards onto the floor and screamed as fire shot down my leg. Erin ran out from our bedroom, startled awake. I tried to get up, but the pain was so intense that I couldn't stop shivering like a wet dog.

"I think my hip is dislocated! Pull my leg!" I screamed, desperate to ease the agony in my hip.

Erin grabbed my foot and pulled. The pain was magnified beyond measure. I came unglued and screamed, "Stop, stop... Ah! Stop! Something's wrong!"

"Let me bring in a chair. I'll help you get up!" she said.

I looked up at her and suddenly realized the horrible truth. "Erin, I can't get up this time."

The tears in my eyes were not from the physical pain, but from the realization that it had finally

happened; I had finally broken my already damaged body. Erin panicked and called the hospital. I lay suffering on the floor of my house for a good hour or more waiting for the ambulance.

An elderly ambulance driver arrived and demanded that I get up and get on the gurney. Writhing in pain by this point, I yelled, "I can't! I can't even move!"

He grabbed me and jerked my hip, insisting that I lift myself off the ground and help. I slapped his hands away in a knee-jerk response to the pain, and he threatened, "If ya don't git up 'n git on this gurney, I'm leavin' without ya!"

Erin cried out, "How's he supposed to get on the gurney! Can't you tell he's hurt? He can't even sit up!"

Just then the owner of the local grocery store saw the lights of the ambulance and stopped to lend a hand. Another friend helped me onto the gurney, then into the ambulance, and rode with me to the hospital, where I waited, and waited. Eventually I was taken in for x-rays.

It had been over three hours since my fall and still no pain medication. A doctor looked at the x-rays and informed me that I'd broken my pelvis into multiple pieces and would need to be transferred to a surgical hospital. I asked for pain meds, but the doctor just looked at me and smiled as he pushed me back into the corner to wait for another ambulance.

Erin arrived and waited with me for another two hours until the second ambulance of the night arrived. The doctor insisted that the driver not strap me in, fearing further injury. For the next two hours I rode with a broken pelvis and a dislocated femur up the winding, steep road to the nearest surgical hospital. Since they couldn't strap me down, the only way I could keep myself from rolling off the gurney was to hold on to the roof rack of the converted minivan with my arm through an open window. Every time the van swayed through a switchback, I felt my femur clanking against my fragmented pelvis.

At the public hospital in San Isidro, I was pushed up against a wall yet again. The emergency room was full of people who thought they might have swine flu. After about fifteen minutes a doctor came and looked at my x-ray. Shocked, he looked up at me and said, "Your pelvis is badly broken. Are you in pain?"

"Please!" I begged. "Give me some morphine or something! I can't take the pain. It's been over six hours since I fell, and I never got pain meds at the other hospital!"

He called two nurses over; one went for the meds and the other checked me in. After a few minutes the doctor walked up and said, "I'm sorry, we're out of pain medication. We'll have to wait until the pharmacy opens at 9:00am." I looked at my watch; it was 4:00am.

Feeling like my head was going to explode, I reached up and grabbed the doctor by the pocket of his scrubs, jerked him down to my level, and said, "Get me to a private hospital with pain meds, now!" The ambulance driver and nurse could see my desperation, so they checked me out and drove me up the road to the private hospital. As soon as we arrived the nurses sprinted into the hospital, returned with a large syringe of morphine, and into the hospital we went.

They braced my legs, and I waited three days for the orthopedic surgeon to arrive. He was friendly and reassuring, and said that everything would be just fine. I went into the surgical room feeling hopeful, as if my suffering was about to end.

The next day, after the surgery, the doctor came to my room with a different outlook. He told me that I had severe muscular dystrophy and osteoporosis. I was overweight, my pelvis was badly broken in several places, and it was his opinion that I would never be able to walk again. He had said the day before that everything would be fine and not to worry. Now he was telling me I would never walk again. Well, this wasn't the first time a doctor had told me that I couldn't walk anymore, so I took it in stride knowing that I would be the one to make that decision.

After the surgery, going back home wasn't an option. Erin had to quickly find a rental house for us near the city so I would have access to regular physical therapy. Our families took turns flying down to help out. Mom came to stay for a few weeks. She cooked my favorite foods and attended to my every need so Erin could leave with the kids and check on the house back down at the beach.

Rasta called early that first week to wish me well, and said he wanted to come see me. He joked with me about the accident and we laughed about having to crap in a bedpan. I told him not to worry. "These doctors are full of it, Man. I'll be back on my feet in no time." We made plans for him to ride up with Erin that Friday. Thinking about his visit distracted me from the pain and gave me something to look forward to.

Thursday morning my phone rang. It was one of my friends – one of Rasta's childhood buddies. I hadn't spoken with him since the accident, and he seemed sad. Trying to lighten the mood, I joked with him, "You're taking this harder than I am!" He got even more quiet, and I asked, "What's wrong, Bro? You sound sad. Don't worry, I'll be alright!"

He started to cry, and a cold chill came over my body. "What's going on, Dude? Tell me now. You're freaking me out! What happened?"

"Something really bad happened, and you're gonna be really upset!" he burst out.

"What? Tell me!" I exclaimed, feeling helpless in my bed.

"It's Rasta, Man... he's been hit by a car. H-he died last night." Crying uncontrollably, overcome by grief, he stammered, "I-I'm sorry!" and hung up.

I handed the phone to Mom and asked for a few minutes alone. She shut the door, and the combination of pain and sorrow were too overwhelming. I began to cry and remember all the times I had spent with Rasta. Unable to understand what was happening, and feeling like my world was crumbling all around me, I cried out, "Why?!"

A presence fell over me, like the gravity of the room had lightened. The stress and pain in my body floated away like I was being given a gift from some unknown source. I lay there in silence, and my misery subsided. A small grin glinted across my face, and I felt that Rasta was with me, giving me peace and an escape from the pain.

The pain returned the next day, and with it my feelings of overwhelming sadness. I'd been dealing with depression and the frustration of having limited control over my body for roughly fourteen years. This was different; it was darker, deeper, and more macabre. I was taking all the prescribed medications – painkillers, anti-inflammatories, and neurological inhibitors – yet nothing seemed to relieve the pain from the nerve damage that had occurred during surgery. It felt as if my right foot and lower leg were being held in a raging brush fire. The burning agony was starting to break me down. I was exhausted and exasperated; sleep had become something I could only daydream about. Delirious most days, I would sleep two or three hours at night only to be awakened by extreme pain.

I lay in bed for six weeks and developed bed sores. Kai had just started walking, and after watching the therapist work with my legs, he started grabbing my foot and shaking it every chance he could get, trying to mimic her. That sent me into a pain panic, which he thought was hilarious, so he did it some more. I could only beg him to stop until Erin would hear the hysteria and come to the rescue.

After six weeks of rigorous rehab, an ultrasound was taken of my pelvis to see if the bones had fused. The doctor told me I could start sitting up for an hour a day and slowly build up from there. I asked him when I could start standing and trying to walk, but he just shook his head and explained that the nerve damage to my foot had caused major foot drop. Combined with all my other complications, walking wasn't a possibility. He told me I needed to get used to my wheelchair.

That was my last appointment with the orthopedic surgeon. I didn't care for his finite attitude towards my recovery, so I decided to recuperate without his guidance. A few weeks later I got to my feet with the help of my therapist, my sister, Erin, and a walker. I stood there, shaking like a newborn deer, unable to pick my foot up off the ground – but it was a start! I was on my feet, even if it took three people to help get me there. From that point I worked on standing up and picking up my feet while standing in place.

Eventually I started taking my first steps down the long path of learning to walk again. After a few weeks I could get up with the help of only two people, and was able to walk into the bathroom and take my first real bath in over two months.

Once I was able to ride in a car, we decided to return home. I had really been looking forward to going home after such a long time away. But the memories of Rasta and my life previous to the accident were staring me down like a prizefighter as soon as I walked in the door. I couldn't get up on my own, use the bathroom, make food, or even get myself a glass of water. Four months had passed since the surgery, and I was still pissing in a bottle and using a bedpan because I couldn't get up on my own. Everywhere I looked, all I saw were memories of Rasta. I saw his big, smiling face; but I couldn't talk to him. I clung to his memory instead of dealing with the life I had lost.

The depression was overwhelming and unrelenting. Wondering if the pain would ever go away, I started thinking that the doctor was right – that I might not recover. These doom-filled thoughts, combined with years of physical and emotional challenges, caught up with me. I was tired of fighting, tired of being angry, and tired of living in pain. I started thinking that maybe Erin and the kids would be better off if I weren't around to burden them with my needs. The Texas tough guy had finally met his match and was ready to throw in the towel.

CHAPTER 11

My Muse

Love is something that can't be measured with any device we have here on earth. It can't be measured because it can't be defined. Love is something we feel, but it's more than that; it's a force so strong that it can inspire change and launch us into different ways of thinking and operating in our world. It's too vast to measure and too powerful to contain, but it is who and what we are at our core.

So many of us are unhappy in our lives because we try to squeeze the love out of others instead of giving love to ourselves. A deep, personal love affair with our self is essential to our well-being, but it's something our society doesn't always embrace or even understand. We have all been taught to look for love and seek love in other people, places, and things. If we can't find someone to love us, then we must be invaluable. But I believe we must first maturate a profound love of ourselves in order to truly understand what love is. Only then can we appreciate the power that it holds in our lives to manifest change.

Erin showed me love and showered me in her love, and I began to realize that I didn't love myself. Through her actions and daily practices, she demonstrated how she loved herself and therefore had the capacity to share her love with me. I, on the other hand, felt hatred and condemnation for myself, and kept myself locked in a cage of self-debilitating anger and rage about my past and present situations. This hate spilled into other areas of my life and caused me to judge and blame others. It didn't matter whether they were friend or foe; I could play judge and jury with everyone. They all came up guilty in my court of self-hate. I denied the good in myself and judged the bad in others. I thought that life was unfair and that others had it in for me. It was easier to blame others for my problems; I didn't understand that I was really passing judgment on myself. Erin made me question my habits. She helped me see that

the less we judge, the more we grow our ability to change. I had been so caught up in the things that were happening to me that I didn't realize I was creating my own negative situations.

I had no love for myself. I thought that love was something you hold in your heart for someone else – that special someone who makes you feel complete. In truth, we must first love ourselves, then allow others into our lives to share in that love.

Erin taught me this through her example and our thought-provoking conversations about the way I functioned in the world. She took the time to care for her needs first so she could be in loving balance. She showed me that being selfish isn't bad; in fact, it's vital to creating a world that we can control. She was the one who determined who and what came into her life. Erin allowed things to be what they were, not judging every single moment as good or bad, but as part of a constant flow called life. It's how we react to our inherent life experiences that determines our outlook on the world that we are creating. In other words, our outer world is only a projection of our inner world.

After my accident and losing my friend Rasta, I felt like I was losing my grip on life; it felt as though

everything was being taken away from me. I wanted to hold on to the things that I perceived as lost, but in reality I was the one who was lost. I was lost in my judgments of the seemingly unchangeable.

One of my biggest frustrations, that I didn't yet realize I had the power to change, was my physical appearance. I was overweight, and my exercise options were limited due to muscular dystrophy and the additional challenge of a broken pelvis. Years before the accident, Erin had tried to get me to address my weight issues. I would always respond in anger and say that she didn't understand. I would argue and say, "How am I going to lose weight when I can't exercise?" I was unwilling to accept change, and sat in judgment of myself for being overweight. I was holding on to the weight because I hated myself for being fat. Even when I tried dieting, I couldn't make any headway.

After the accident Erin said to me, "Now you're going to lose weight because you don't have a choice. I'm changing your diet, and you might as well accept it because there's nothing you can do about it." She continued, "Just give up control because you're going to eat what I bring you since you can't get up anyway."

I was so depressed and tired of fighting that I didn't even argue and I didn't judge what was happening. In fact, I just felt blessed that I had a wife who cared enough to help. Because of this, I accepted and understood that I needed to make a change if I was ever going to get back on my feet.

Erin and I then began eating a healthy, vegetarian diet of mostly green raw foods with high alkaline. She made sure that I drank plenty of water, and tea instead of coffee. Whenever I felt the need to eat and complained of hunger, she would say, "Drink some water. Your body's trying to tell you that it needs more water." I started to realize she was right as I lost weight. I was letting go of judgments about myself and the food I was eating. I loved myself enough to release the weight that I had been holding on to. It was easier to move around, and I started feeling hopeful again.

The more I loved myself, the better I felt, and feeling better made me want to care for myself even more. I began to crave healthy food and an abundance of water. I drank four liters of water a day and found that I ate less and less food. Over the course of ten months I lost seventy pounds without even exercising. All I did was allow my body to come into its natural, balanced state.

Now the challenge was to get off the pain meds and out of the bed. I was in a weird place; I felt good about losing the weight, but I was still stuck in the deep depression that had taken hold many years earlier. I was living in a state of stress and anxiety, constantly worried about what was happening to my body. Many days I would just cry, or try to sleep the day away. I saw my life as a struggle – a fight to hold on to the little bit of life I had left. The depression was even more crippling than the MD or my broken pelvis.

Erin had finally seen enough of my self-loathing. Standing over the bed with her hands firmly at her hips she said, "It's time to get up and get out of this bed. I'm tired of seeing you just lying around depressed and feeling sorry for yourself. This isn't you, and not the life I want for me and our kids. And if you don't stop soon, I'm leaving. I can't stay here and watch you let your life pass you by from a bed. What kind of example are you setting right now?" She walked out of the room, slamming the door.

I would love to say that I pulled myself up at that moment, but the truth is that I cried for the rest of the day. I felt like I was losing everything. Then

I realized that I'd do anything to keep my family together. I decided that I could deal with the physical challenges and the pain. I knew that Erin was trying to motivate me, and I also knew that she was serious about leaving if I didn't change my attitude. I couldn't accept losing my family. And for the first time in my life I realized that I was in control of what I allowed to happen to me.

The next few months were painful and psychologically challenging. How was I going to overcome the obstacles in my path to recovery? After the surgery, I couldn't control my leg or foot. My toes were curled and pointed down, and I couldn't bring them back to a normal position. After a few months of rehab, I was only able to barely move my foot slightly inward towards my left ankle. The only feeling in my foot was a raw, burning sensation that felt like broken glass scraping over my skin.

Losing weight was one thing, but how was I ever going to overcome nerve damage and major foot drop? I was scared and discouraged. And the meds I was taking were clouding my mind and giving me false feedback about my pain.

The first issue was my addiction to pain meds, again. I needed to stop taking them so that I could trust my body and reconnect my body-brain feedback. This was harder and more painful than I anticipated. I thought that since I had kicked an addiction to pain meds once, it would be easy to do it again. I was wrong. Erin and I fought continuously over whether or not I needed the meds. I would wait double the time required, and finally cave in to the pain and take some more.

One day Erin drove to the pharmacy for a refill, and when she came back she said, "That's it. You're done after this round. You'll just keep taking this forever if I keep refilling it. These are the last pain pills I'm bringing home."

I was so angry at Erin at that moment, but I said nothing. I was like a whipped puppy dog looking for a place to curl up and hide with my sorrows. The next day, after my emotions had settled, I knew that Erin was right and that things had to change if I was ever going to get my life back. I made almost two weeks of meds last for about a month, and ultimately stopped taking them before I ran out just to prove to myself that it was my choice.

The next few months were taxing, both mentally and physically. I did my rehab every day, but it seemed like I was stuck in the same place. I was making progress, but the measure of progress can sometimes be painful and deceiving. I was no longer using a bedpan, but now Erin had to come and help lift me off the toilet after I was done in the bathroom.

I had to let go, accept help, and acknowledge that I was a tired and broken soul in need of major healing. The months dragged by, and little by little I started helping out in the kitchen again. This was my domain. I loved to cook, and it helped me relax and focus my attention on something other than my problems. It was hard to believe that I hadn't cooked anything for myself in ten months. I was eager to get back in the kitchen, but quickly realized I needed help to do even the simplest things.

From the kitchen window I'd look at the car and think about driving. I enjoyed cooking, but I loved to drive even more. I told Erin that I wanted to start driving again. She just looked at me and half smiled. She asked, "Do you really think you should be driving a car? Would you want me to drive a car if I couldn't control my leg?" Her questions brought me to tears, because I didn't want to answer. I started asking friends of mine to take me for rides, and rode along with Erin when she ran errands. I was working up my endurance for sitting in the car and riding on bumpy roads with unexpected stops.

Finally, after many conversations and arguments about the safety of myself and others, I decided I was ready. I called a friend, and he came right over to help. It had been eighteen months since I had been behind the wheel. I was nervous and scared. What if I couldn't do it and my driving days were over?

I pulled out of the driveway with my left foot on the brake and my right foot on the gas – and with the parking brake on, too, just for good measure. It was a shaky start. I didn't feel comfortable with only one good leg, and it was the wrong leg, too. I started thinking, "Why couldn't it have happened differently?" Then I realized that way of thinking wasn't going to help me drive again.

I drove around the little village every day for the next few weeks and figured out how to best use my arms and legs to compensate for the limited strength and range of motion in my leg. After experimenting with different techniques I found that using my right foot on the gas and my left foot on the brake was the best and most effective way to drive. The true test was to take my car onto the dreaded highway to see if I could do it all fast enough to feel safe driving with passengers – or myself for that matter. Just before the two-year anniversary of breaking my pelvis, I was driving my family down the highway to our daily events.

After a few months I felt more comfortable and hopeful that I'd get my life back to normal. It was then that Erin approached me, not about my physical healing, but about my mental and spiritual state of mind. She said my spirit was broken and that I was living in a world of "what if," confused by the dreams I held in my heart and the physical reality that limited my ability to realize those dreams. She knew that I was giving up and checking out. Sure, I had recovered a bit since the accident, but she could tell I wasn't happy and that I'd lost a part of myself somewhere along the way.

"I know that you're still depressed. You're trying to act like things are better, or that you're okay with everything that's happened, but you're not. You're not yourself."

I angrily responded, "What am I? Who am I? Just some guy who gets a pension because my life is fucked up! I get a handout from the government because there's something wrong with me! Nobody sees me for who I am. They only see a big dude with a walker and nobody wants to understand because it's too scary to think that it could happen to them!"

It was at this moment that I realized *I* was scared – afraid of what I had become. I had no idea who I was or what I was. I had been full of rage – a hatred that had clouded my ability to see my true self. I couldn't love others or allow myself to be forgiven because I hadn't fully accepted my life and the choices I had made.

CHAPTER 12

The Golden Vine

When we feel thrust into an unwelcome situation, we usually do what our culture has taught us: resist, shut down, blame, and deflect. But these reactions only put our bodies into survival mode and create heightened states of stress and anxiety. Acceptance and surrender are two things that I had been taught to resist, and it's especially hard to accept things into our lives that we don't want in the first place, like pain and disease. How do you know when to fight back and when to accept? Where is the line between struggle and surrender? The battle I fought with my body – to continue walking when others told me I couldn't – had only led to a terrible fall in my own home, the further degeneration of my body, and chronic depression.

I finally realized that there was nothing left to do but surrender to muscular dystrophy, accept my life, and stop looking for immediate solutions. I was on the road to self-discovery, but it was a long, winding path, and it was easy to lose my way. I needed as much help as I could get, but the whole idea of love and forgiveness was a new concept. Soon after making the decision to surrender to what was, people began to show me love and offer guidance when I least expected it.

While having lunch at one of my favorite restaurants one day, I ran into a friend – an ex-hippie-surfer I was always happy to see. "Whoa! What happened to you, Bro? What's up with the walker?"

"Oh man, I fell in my house just walking to bed one night and broke my pelvis."

"Well, how long 'till you get rid of the walker?" he asked.

I hesitated, then told him the grim prognosis: "The doctors said that I'd never walk again, so I don't know – I'm just taking it one day at a time."

He refused to accept my answer and told me about a naturopathic doctor he was sure could help me. "His name is Herman, and he lives only a couple hours away. Maybe we can go together sometime?"

This was an interesting idea, and I appreciated his concern, but I couldn't seriously believe there was anyone who could help me. I left the restaurant and shook my friend's hand without taking down the doctor's number.

About a month or so afterward I was in the grocery store with Kai. A looming, gruff-looking man peered down at me and said abruptly, "You look like a young guy. What the hell are you doing with a walker?"

Strangely refreshed by this stranger's honesty and bluntness, I told him about the accident. Like most people, he wondered, "But how could you break your pelvis so badly just from a simple fall?"

I didn't like to tell people about the MD and avoided it by talking only about the accident. I didn't want their pity, or to label myself with the disease. But for one of the first times in my life, I told a total stranger the truth: that I had MD, which had caused me to develop osteoporosis.

He looked upset and even angry about my story. As it turned out, he, too, had been in the Navy, and we found a common bond. After swapping a few nautical stories, he opened his wallet, pulled out a business card, and handed it to me. "This is a naturopathic doctor who lives in the area. I've been seeing him for a while now, and he can do some amazing things! Take this card, go home, and call him today to make an appointment."

When I saw the name "Herman" printed on the card, I went home, made the appointment, and arranged to carpool with my surfer friend.

From the moment I met Herman, I could tell there was something special about him. His bright, crystal-like eyes were piercing, yet calm, and he overflowed with loving acceptance and grace. With no claims that he could heal or cure me, he said, "If you are up to the challenge of regaining your health, I'm here to help you on that journey. You're the one who must decide how much you can recover. It's not up to me."

His medical treatments consisted of Vitamin C and Impletol injections. But we spent most of the time talking. He asked me about my childhood, and I cried profusely as I told him every detail. After the first visit I could already feel a change inside me. It was more than just the treatment; I had released my old thoughts, clearing a path for a new way of thinking.

These new thoughts and ideas were coming at me so fast that I started journaling to keep track of them. I had spent so much time depressed and angry that I couldn't believe that all of these optimistic ideas were coming out of me! The more I wrote, the more I integrated the ideas into my life. A new pattern was forming that would lead to experiences I never would have imagined.

After carpooling with my surfer friend to Herman's office for a few months, I felt comfortable enough to ask my friend about a book I had been reading on shamanic medicine. "Do you know anything about ayahuasca?" I asked.

He turned and looked at me suspiciously. "What do you know about it?"

"I've been reading about it, and I'm wondering if it would help me on my journey," I explained.

On our way home we talked about ayahuasca, a traditional Amazonian spiritual medicine that has powerful psychedelic properties. But I soon forgot about the whole thing and moved on. After a few weeks my phone rang, and my surfer friend told me to start detoxing my body, giving me specific instructions on how to do so.

Laughing at his abrupt, random request, I asked, "Why?"

He said, "We're doing an ayahuasca ceremony at my house this Friday! You're in, right?"

I was nervous and a little shocked, but answered, "Yes, of course! What time should I be there and where do you live?"

When I arrived, things immediately became weird in a kind of full-circle, synchronistic way. My surfer friend introduced me to the facilitator. As soon as I met him, I had a feeling that I knew him. After a half hour or so of talking, I realized that he had stayed at the hotel in Ojochal that Erin and I had run four years earlier. He laughed when I told him how we knew each other, and we reminisced about those first few months in the jungle.

Then the sun painted the Pacific Ocean with a golden hue and we began our ceremony. Over the previous few months I had read many accounts of ayahuasca, and I was a little nervous. I didn't know exactly what to expect, but I was open to the experience and willing to go wherever I was led. We drank our first round and settled in. I chose the couch, and as I lay back and relaxed into the moment, my mind began to wander. I recounted past experiences with LSD and psychedelic mushrooms, recalling how they seemed to roll in hard, overwhelm my mind with visual stimuli, and shut off the constant banter of my own thoughts. Just as my curiosity was running wild, the facilitator came up to me, placed his hand softly on my shoulder, and said, "You're lost in your thoughts. It's time to drink another round and relax a bit more."

I sat up, drank the next shot of yagé – the local name for ayahuasca, and settled back down into stillness. By this time it was very dark, and the only light was a candle off in the distance by the front door. Within a few minutes I could feel a familiar tug on my brain. The naturally occurring DMT, or dimethyltryptamine, in the "golden vine" was inviting me to take a trip, but this was different from the psychedelic experiences I'd had before. It wasn't cold and mechanical. It was a warm embrace – an invitation to come along on a journey. And I agreed to follow.

When I closed my eyes I saw darkness blacker than a moonless night in the heart of the jungle – not the blackness of night, but a darkness of hate and rage. It was an empty, barren, cold, and cruel world, devoid of love and light, and I began to realize that this was my mind, my world, my creation. Then I heard a loving voice say, "Let go. This is not who you are. Let go!"

I asked the faceless voice, "Why is it so dark, and why do I feel afraid?"

Right away I heard a response: "Let go. Just forgive and let go!"

At that moment I felt tears squeezing through my clenched eyelids. I could see and understand that all the rage and anger had turned into an abyss of blackness and disease. I was being shown my internal darkness and how it was consuming my life.

I opened my eyes and looked at the candle in the distance, desperate for some kind of light to flow into my awareness. The flame slowly grew until it became a single ray of light that came towards me. It felt familiar and comforting. As I concentrated on the light, it moved closer and then drew back a bit before moving in again for what felt like a closer inspection. The light crept towards me until it was only a few feet away, and then suddenly it was gone.

At this point I needed some air, so I went outside. As I gazed up at the stars, my body felt the need to purge the blackness. I had barely eaten for a week, but the amount of material that came heaving out of my mouth felt equal to the darkness of my thoughts.

I went inside and settled back onto the couch, and the facilitator offered me another shot of yagé, which was much harder to choke down than the first two. I closed my eyes again, but the image had changed, and the darkness was gone. All I could see was what appeared to be twisted ropes, and I immediately heard that familiar, faceless voice saying, "Let go!"

As I relaxed into the vision quest, I realized that I could ask questions of this voice, and it seemed to be guiding me. Of course I first asked how to heal myself from muscular dystrophy, but the response was simply, "Let go." Then I asked how to forgive my past and the people who had hurt me, and again the voice from the golden vine said, "Let go." The more questions I asked, the more I understood that I was holding on to these thoughts and trapping myself in negative situations through my own inability to let go of the past and move on.

The night went on, and I asked many more questions. Each time the response was an ever-loving voice begging me to "Let go."

After a few hours, the facilitator stopped singing and drumming and started to perform healing work on myself and the others. He walked up to me and placed his hand softly on the side of my head. As he did, I could see and feel his hand inside of my head. It was like he was in my mind, and the colors suddenly changed to warm hues of orange and yellow. I could feel the calming effects of his touch. He moved on to the next person, so I closed my eyes again to relax. Again I saw the twisting ropes, but as I looked closer I realized they were DNA strands. More important, I knew it was *my* DNA. Now the message was louder and more forceful. I wasn't asking any questions, but I was being told with emphasis to "Let go!"

I began to understand what I was being shown and how it related to the message. The more I relaxed and let go, the more clearly I could see the DNA strands and how they formed a ladder to my healing. If I wanted to climb out of my past, I would have to let go and move on. I would have to forgive myself, my body, and everyone who had hurt me. Once I decided to listen and let go, the inner light came on

and I was shown the ladder that had always been there – the one that could lead me to my salvation.

Our facilitator came around one last time and offered more ayahuasca, but something inside of me had already opened up and I knew I was done. I kindly refused the last shot and got up to go outside to watch the sun rise over the mountains to the east. While I sat there, feeling relaxed and renewed, I listened to the bursting sounds of the waking jungle and was thankful for the experience. Closing my eyes, I felt the blazing sun on my face and grinned.

Then I felt a cool shadow cross my face and I opened my eyes. "What's up, Cosmic Wizard?" There was our facilitator with a glass of fresh-squeezed orange juice and a smile. He handed me the glass and we talked about the experiences we had shared through the night.

He was deeply concerned about some of the things he'd seen while working on me during the ceremony. He recommended that I see a shaman friend of his to participate in a soul-retrieval ceremony. He explained, "Shamans believe that when we experience trauma, our souls become fragmented and the pieces fall out of our bodies. Then we feel loss, sadness, and depression over the parts of ourselves that we can't seem to find. The shaman can help you find the pieces and start putting your life back together."

After the night I had just experienced, I didn't need more explanation. I didn't even ask how he knew so much about me and my past when I hadn't told him about it. I just understood and believed that he knew, so I took the number and agreed to go.

When I got home, Erin could tell that I had been through a transformational experience. But before I could tell her the details, she insisted I answer a couple of strange questions. "Were you on a couch last night, lying down? Was there a blanket and pillow on the floor next to you, where someone had been lying? Was the blanket dark blue?" Her questions were shocking, because the answer to all of them was yes, but she had never been inside the house.

I sat down at the bar in our kitchen and she continued. "Last night I was thinking about you and wondering if you were okay. I wanted to see you, so I went outside to sit in the hammock and closed my eyes. Suddenly I wasn't in the hammock anymore. I could see the inside of a house, but I wasn't walking. It was like I was floating! As I moved closer, I saw you lying on a brown couch, but I couldn't see your legs. Then as I looked closer, I saw you had a blanket over you and your legs were resting on the arm of the couch. I looked back at you, and the couch started to change in shape and color. It became an old, Victorian style couch. Then a hard, leather couch. Suddenly I panicked and realized I wasn't in the hammock anymore, so I left the room and opened my eyes!"

Now I was the one freaking out. Erin had just described to me the exact layout of a room she had never seen and the position in which I had been lying for most of the night. She had even known the color of the couch and floor pillows, and yes, my fellow journeyers had been sitting and lying on the floor pillows next to the coffee table near to me. The craziest part was that when I asked her what time it was when she experienced this, she said it was 9:30 or 10:00, which was the same time that I saw the candle emitting the strange ray of light that seemed to cautiously approach me.

Excited by the mystery of it all, the whole experience came rushing back and I shared every detail with her. Everything had come full circle in less than twenty-four hours. I had seen and experienced true connection, and I wanted to "let go." This small-town, ex-Navy country boy was ready to call the shaman.

CHAPTER 13

Soul Flight

I don't know how I got to this place, but it looks familiar. I'm standing on a high mountain ridge in the rainforest overlooking the broad expanse of the ocean. Behind me is the vibrant green jungle that captures my endearment. Suddenly I realize I'm in another world — an ancient world devoid of technology and chaos — the spirit world. I tell myself to go back to the earthen hut where the ceremony is going on without me. I see myself from behind, and I'm standing on the front porch of the shaman's hut watching the setting sun. I reach out to touch myself on the shoulder with my hand and realize that I'm not in my body; it's as if there are two of me. And when my hand falls softly upon my own shoulder in front of me – Boom!

I opened my eyes and the shaman, Sabina, was breathing deeply, lying next to me in her little dome-shaped mud hut. My mind started to race, trying to make sense of what had just happened. The deep, rhythmic drumming that had held me in the trance had stopped. As I lay in silence, my thoughts wandered to Sabina's words when I had first arrived.

"Have you ever done a shamanic ceremony in the past, other than your recent ayahuasca journey?" she had asked me, lighting a bundle of dried sage.

"No. Why do you ask?"

"Well, there's something about you that I don't understand. You told me that you've had muscular dystrophy since 1995, but your soul is intact. Your spirit is so big it's filling up this entire room; and furthermore it's centered, and strongly connected with your body."

All I could think to say was, "Cool. What does that mean?"

"I don't know, but I think you're more powerful than you realize. It's very important that you stay here with me when we do the ceremony." Then she lit incense and pulled out her drums.

Where does she think I'll go? I thought to myself as she began to drum. *It took the help of two people to get me in this place!*

Sabina opened her eyes after a few minutes and asked if I was ready to hear what she had seen on her journey. I was having trouble understanding my experience and was eager to hear what she had to say.

She smiled and said, "I have been doing these ceremonies for years now, and I have never heard a *voice* in the spirit world. I'm an eagle on my journeys, and usually I'm only guided by animals and people."

Now sitting crossed-legged in front of me, she went on to explain, "The voice first guided me to a desert, and as I flew over the desert, I saw a huge fire and was told to fly into it. Upon entering the flames, I encountered a large sword with a jeweled handle and the voice said that it was yours and that you would need it back to continue on your journey."

As she spoke I felt tears flow like a cascading waterfall down the right side of my face, but she continued. "Next the voice led me to the ocean, and it was at that moment that I saw a gigantic blue whale and realized that he was the one guiding me on this journey. I asked the whale why he was helping me and he said that he was your power spirit. I suddenly understood why your spirit was so big and filled the room when you came into my home. The whale asked me to follow him to the ocean floor, where we entered a cave. There was an old chest, and inside was the most luminescent pearl. The whale said it was yours; it was something that you had lost and he had kept it safe for you. And he gave it to me.

"We left the cave and swam towards the dancing lights that pierced the sea. Once we reached the surface, I asked your blue whale if he was ready to help you on your healing journey. He explained that he had left because of the abuse and torment that he could no longer bear. I told him that you were no longer living under such strain and that you seemed at peace and could use his strength and guidance on your journey. He agreed to come back and help you, and pointed me in the direction of a man standing behind a black veil.

"Usually the person behind a veil is the person who has been the most hurtful to the person in the ceremony. They stand behind the veil because they're ashamed of the things they have done and don't want to be seen. I explained to the man that you were on a healer's journey and that you needed help, and he said he wanted to help you. Then he handed me a metal box. I opened the box and inside were three old, hand-painted army men made of nickel. He said that he wanted you to have them and that you would know what they were."

I had no clue what these metal army men were or what they were supposed to mean to me. I was confused about the details, but I was certain that the man behind the veil was Dad.

The pillow supporting my head was serving as a sponge, soaking up the uncontrollable tears that were springing up and out of my eyes. I said, "I understand parts of what you're saying, but I don't understand the symbolism of everything you brought back for me."

Sabina said, "Go home and write it all down. Speak with Erin about it and soon you will have more understanding." She invited me to come back to her house in a few days to learn more about journeying.

On the way home I felt a wholeness that had seemed distant for so long. It was like wearing a brand new unwashed shirt. It felt good, but I was itching to break it in and be more comfortable with these long-lost feelings.

When I got home I told Erin every detail of the experience. I explained the shamanic concept of the fragmented soul and how the journey into the spirit world is a quest to find the missing pieces. "I understood the sword and the blue whale," I said. "But the rest is a mystery to me."

She asked, "What does the sword mean to you?"

I recounted all of my thoughts from the drive home. "The sword represents my lack of power and inability to stand up for myself, to fend off unwanted attacks from the people intent on hurting me. The blue whale is a symbol of great size and strength. I haven't been expressing myself in a confident and powerful way. I've been shrinking myself down and becoming quieter, smaller, and more depressed over the years. The blue whale also represents knowledge and wisdom. I haven't been making wise choices over the last few years concerning my mental or physical health. But the luminous pearl and the metal box of army men didn't make sense to me."

Erin grabbed a piece of paper and drew a sketch of the items Sabina had brought back, all arranged together like presents under a tree. When she was done, she gave it to me and said, "I think I know what the other pieces mean if you want me to tell you."

She continued, "The pearl was buried at the bottom of the ocean, locked away in a dark chest, right? I think this represents your self-esteem – the love for yourself that you've forgotten and buried. It's a symbol of the brilliant light you can give off when you choose to be who you really are.

"The box of antique army men that your dad gave the shaman represents the childhood that was stolen from him. That's why the army men are old and hand-painted, from the era when he was a kid. He wants to give you back the childhood he stole from you."

All I could do was cry, again. She was right, and I thought how blessed I was to have such a special person as Erin for my wife. I kept the drawing and wrote down the meaning of the symbolic pieces in my journal.

After a few days I went back to Sabina's farm, excited to learn more about journeying. She gave me an MP3 player and a set of headphones and explained the process. "The drumming will start slowly. This is when you set your intention on where you want to go and what questions you have. Then the drumming will speed up to a faster, rhythmic pace. Once that happens you will find yourself at an access point, some path that you can use to get to the lower, middle, or upper realms of the spirit world." Then she told me where she wanted me to go and what to look for.

When the slow drum pounded in my ears, I found my mind wandering just like it had when I first started my meditation practice. I tried to relax and clear my thoughts, but more thoughts kept distracting me. Then the fast drum kicked in, and I was off to a large, open field with tall, dry grasses swaying in the wind around a large hole. This was an access point Sabina had told me I would find. I entered the hole with my intention to explore the lower realm, and after a short ten minutes of journeying, I heard the callback drum and returned.

I pulled down the headphones and said, "I went to the lower realm like you told me, but I'm not sure if I actually went there or it was just my imagination. I didn't encounter any animals or people. It was just a vast and beautiful landscape. Maybe I didn't do it right."

Sabina laughed and said, "When a shaman trained me to journey I said the same thing to her. I thought it was just my imagination carrying me away. You will see in time, as different encounters and lessons are given to you in the spirit world, that it is nothing that you could have imagined. Are you ready to go again?"

"Yeah, I think so," I said.

This time she lit incense and stepped out of the room. Before she left, she told me where to go and what to look for, and said, "If you encounter any animals or people, you should try to speak with them." She put on the thirty-minute drumming track, smiled, and walked away.

This time it was much easier. I went straight to the field with the gaping hole, and like a flash I was back in the spirit world.

> I'm standing in a wide meadow full of wildflowers and tall grass. Verdant trees sway in the wind off in the distance. As I look to the trees, a large male deer emerges and walks towards me. I try to speak with the deer as I inch my way towards him. When the distance between us is no more than a few feet, the deer looks deeply into my eyes, then turns and runs over the horizon into the forest. Without hesitation I give chase, accelerating at an unworldly pace on the heels of my guide.
>
> It's amazing – running, jumping, and darting through the woods! Then, unexpectedly,

the deer pulls his head up, digs in his hooves, and slides to a stop. I stop only a few feet from the cliff that he had anticipated. The ridge comes to a point, and there are two waterfalls cascading down both sides of the cliff into a ravine so deep that the water dissipates into clouds, obstructing the valley view below.

Looking into the deer's eyes I ask, "What are you trying to show me?" I hear his voice in my head, and his only response is, "Jump!" I give him a puzzled look and retort, "Jump where?" Again he urges, "Just jump!" Full of confidence, and excited to see what will follow, I leap over the edge and descend rapidly into the mist of water and clouds. At once I'm engulfed in a cool fog of confusion. I feel as if I've stopped falling. Just as this thought enters my mind, a bald eagle appears in my peripheral vision. It swoops in close and looks me straight in the eye, and its voice rings in my head, "Follow me."

I'm not falling – I'm flying! We shoot out of the mist like jets at Mach speed. I can see the mountains behind me, the vast forest below, and the sapphire ocean on the distant horizon. We take a sharp turn and head for a cluster of trees on the ridge next to the waterfall. From this vantage point we can see

everything in the distance. I take a moment to look around, and then wonder, "How am I doing all of this?" I look down and see large, yellowish feet and sharp talons. Then I look over at my arms, but instead see feathers and wings. I've transformed into an eagle! Before I can fully adjust to my new form, I hear a booming crackle that rattles the sky and shakes our perch.

A white-hot flash of lightning strikes the forest below, and it's transformed into a raging inferno. When I turn towards the eagle to ask what's happening, he springs from the tree. I instinctively spread my wings and follow. We race over the firestorm, observing the destruction of the forest. I feel anxiety and fear that everything will be lost. We perch in some trees a safe distance from the fire, and I say, "I don't understand. The entire forest is being destroyed!" Just as these words leave my mind, the eagle turns my attention to the storm that had started the fire. We rocket out of the tree and into the looming thunderhead above us. We fly straight up until we pierce the clouds, and then drift in the calm, cool air above the turbulence.

The storm rolls over the blazing landscape and extinguishes the uncontrollable flames. We

glide back down through the dark clouds over the charred wasteland. I witness the growth of the new forest rising from the ashes of its destruction. It's like watching a high-speed time-lapse nature film. First the new trees spring from the dry, baked earth and grow at an accelerated rate, followed by the grasses and mushrooms. Then the animals return to feed on the new vegetation and rebuild their nests and burrows. Everything that had been destroyed is renewed, and the new forest seems even more vibrant and alive than before. The storm and the destruction that had laid waste to this pristine wonderland are a distant memory in just a matter of minutes.

My companion and I land in a large tree in the new growth of the forest. I look into the eagle's eyes and say, "I don't understand. What does this all mean?" For the first time the eagle looks deep into my eyes and speaks to my mind, "You know what this all means!"

I hear the sound of the slow drum calling me back, but I don't want to leave. I'm beginning to realize that these two worlds are connected but the answers to one world are contained in the other. I thank my guide for the most sacred journey of my life and open my eyes.

When the shaman returned to the room, I was bursting with excitement and I couldn't believe what had just transpired. I told her, "I'm convinced that wasn't my imagination. There's no way I could've just made that up. I feel a connection between this world and the spirit world. Each time the eagle and I took off in flight, I could feel the rush of the breeze and the airflow pick up around me in this world. The incense you lit began to smell like a burning forest instead of nag champa."

"So what does it all mean to you?" she asked.

I tried my best to explain. "I think it means that in order to build a new and better world for myself, I'm supposed to go through these challenges. My old world and life had to burn; in fact it needed to burn down so that I could create a new, healthier world. Just as nature found beauty in the devastation of the forest, it used the chaos to build a better, more vibrant world."

Sabina looked at me, smiled, and said, "I knew you would enjoy this."

CHAPTER 14

An Open Mind

When we accept who we are and allow our "true self" to emerge, our powers of intuition and instinct are amplified. We can open doors to the soul, proceed with self-confidence, and gain a deeper understanding of our life's purpose. The trick is letting go! The more I worked on myself and practiced letting go of my old beliefs, the stronger my internal voice became. It became so loud, in fact, that I agreed to attend a reiki class that I really had no interest in. My friend Victoria asked if I'd like to sign up, and when my instinct told me to say yes, I grudgingly obeyed.

Once you start on a healing journey, your consciousness and perceptions change. These

changes can't always be explained by common logic or scientific facts, and can cause confusion or even fear. The confusion comes from believing that you live in a world that is fixed or normal, based in logic and explanation. Fear occurs when you realize you've been chasing an illusion, and that there's more to this world than what we can see. Logic, reason, and fear of the unknown had almost kept me from experiencing the magic and mystery of the unexplainable.

Just a few days after agreeing to the reiki class, I was picking up my kids from school and noticed an eccentric, colorfully dressed lady sitting across the street at my friend's restaurant. I asked my friend about her, and she said, "Solaya is a psychic and tarot card reader. She'll be here at the restaurant over the next few weeks, and I was thinking you might like to see her."

I decided to trust my instinct and made an appointment. When I arrived at the restaurant a few days later, I was overwhelmed by her beautiful smile and her energy of loving joy. There was something familiar and yet very mysterious about Solaya. She had long silver hair and the deepest amber eyes I had ever seen. She spoke formal English with a thick, exotic French accent.

She invited me to sit down at a small table under the shade of a lemon tree. On the table was a stack of tarot cards that had been fanned out like a deck of playing cards. As I looked at her and the cards, I asked myself, *What are you doing here?* followed by, *Do you really think this lady and these cards have the answers to your questions?*

Just as I completed these thoughts, I looked up from the cards to notice her smiling at me and saying, "You have never done anything like this before, have you?"

"No. I always thought this stuff was a little silly," I admitted to her.

"Why?" she asked.

"I just don't see how a few cards can tell me anything about my life and why I'm struggling with depression and disease."

Solaya just smiled, slowly gathered up her cards, and put them into a blue felt bag and tied it shut with its golden rope. Then she asked me if I would tell her a little bit about my life and what I was currently going through. I told her about my past and how I had recently started seeing shamans and other healers. I informed her that since I had started this journey, things were happening to me that I couldn't explain or even understand.

The more questions she asked me, the more I realized that I was following some unseen path and that new non-physical things were coming forth to help me on my journey. After a few more questions, she asked if I would do something with her before the tarot card reading. I said yes, and she took my hand and asked me to close my eyes and breathe three deep breaths with her. I felt myself relaxing into the moment with my eyes closed. Startled by the voice and strange accent that I was now hearing, my eyes popped open. I looked at Solaya, and she seemed to be listening intently to something or someone else. She had her eyes closed in deep concentration.

Immediately I knew that something unexplainable was going on. The first thing she said blew my mind: "You've been asked to take a reiki class and you should do it." She was suddenly speaking better English, and her word usage had changed to an American style of speaking that included slang words. As if reading my mind, she added, "I know you don't want to take the class and touch people with your hands, but it's time to let people back into your life."

She continued, saying, "You're confused by all the changes in your life right now, and you can feel something around you or behind you. These changes are happening because you want them to happen on a deep, subconscious level. You've been through a lot of physical and emotional pain, and your ailments have brought you insight and understanding about healing. You are a healer, and you are here to teach others how to heal themselves because you understand something about healing from your past experiences and suffering."

Then she opened her eyes and peered into mine. I noticed that her deep, amber-brown eyes now had small specks like gold leaf in them, turning and rotating like moons orbiting a planet. My entire body was now covered in goosebumps, and she looked over my head and said with a smile, "The reason you feel different and guided to do this work now is because you have a spirit attached to you. He was a holistic doctor in his past life, and he has come to help you and wants you to help him also. He says that you understand that healing requires joining the spirit, heart, mind, and body."

I quickly stopped her and said, "I don't want to be a healer. And I don't want to work on other people

and their problems even if I do know these things about healing!"

To which she replied, smiling, "You don't have to do anything, but if you choose to follow your path, you will be supported and find success. You chose this path before you ever came into this life, and everything up to this point has been there to support you in your life's purpose! If you decide to do something else, that's fine, but you will feel more content and whole if you follow and trust your true path."

She then closed her eyes and asked me to breathe with her again. I did, and when she opened her eyes, everything was "normal." She took out her tarot cards, shuffled the deck, and asked me to choose eleven cards.

I was amazed further by her reading of the cards I had chosen, which reinforced what she had already told me. She could see that I had been to design school and loved art, but that I had abandoned my artistic expression due to frustration. She also saw that I was at a point of major transition and transformation, one that would lead me further down the path of healing and discovering my purpose.

I left that day feeling confused but oddly content, and a little more excited about the reiki class coming up. I didn't have all the answers I was looking for, but for the first time in my life I was excited about the mystery of the unknown.

The next week I began my reiki course, and I was, again, a little skeptical of all of the talk about energy and allowing energy to flow and be transferred from one person to another. I found the instructor, Victoria, to be very practical and grounded, which made me feel more comfortable about the whole idea.

When she began to speak about her experiences with reiki, its healing effects, and visually seeing the energy flow, I thought to myself, *Bullshit! You can't convince me that you had green energy flowing from your hands over a patient in the hospital!* I wanted to leave, but I had already paid for the course and there were some other interesting people there, so I stayed.

We covered techniques and the placement of hands on the body. We did guided meditations, and I could feel the energy in the room. Many of the people in the class wept during the meditations and said that they could see and feel the energy around them.

That first day we received reiki *attunements*, yet another thing that I thought was a bunch of malarkey. I watched the entire class go before me. They sat in a chair over some crystals and the instructor waved her hands around over each person's body, said some mantras, and voilà, you were infused with reiki energy.

After we had all received our attunements, we moved over to the massage tables and practiced reiki on each other. I chose to be the first on the table, and my partner, a reiki master, performed reiki on me. I felt very calm and relaxed, and the longer I was on the table, the more I could feel what I can only describe as a warm, flowing blanket wrapped around me.

Then the instructor said time was up and that we should switch positions. As I opened my eyes, I felt as if I had just awakened from a long and restful sleep. It was hard to get up off the table, and I felt a little out of sorts.

I stood over my reiki master partner and felt very nervous and self-conscious. I didn't like the idea of touching other people. I asked the instructor if we had to touch the person, and she said we could just hold our hands above the person and allow the energy to flow from our hands into them. I closed my eyes and began to hold my hands over my partner. Just as I held my hands over her, the wind started to blow through the open windows and swirl around the room. I felt a strong sensation like I was floating on ripples of water. When I opened my eyes, I looked down at my partner and her dress was flowing and rippling like a flag on a gusty day. Then her skin moved in unison with her rippling, flowing dress.

I thought I was losing my mind. This wasn't really happening... or was it? When we were called to finish I asked her, "What did you feel while I was performing reiki on you?"

"It felt like I was floating in water, riding on the ripples of the surface," she answered.

"Are you serious?" I exclaimed.

"Yes. It was very nice and relaxing. You have a real gift for reiki," she said.

I went home that night excited, but confounded. After all, I didn't believe in any of that stuff; I was just giving it a try to see if it helped me focus my energy. Now my whole reality was changing. I was beginning to believe in things that all my logic and reasoning couldn't explain. I was starting to believe what I was seeing, which helped me begin to see what I had always known in my heart. The more I opened myself to the mystery, the more magical my life was becoming.

The next day I returned, eager to receive my second attunement and learn more about reiki. We covered more material and did some meditations, and then we got our reiki II attunement and began to practice with our partners again.

The first session was hands-on, with our partners seated in chairs in front of us. I sat down first and again felt the now familiar feeling of relaxation and tranquility. When I opened my eyes, I again felt extremely rested and a bit out of it.

We switched positions, and I asked my partner if she was ready to begin. As I placed my hands on her shoulders, she jolted as if she'd been struck by lightning. I asked if she was okay and she just turned her head towards me with her eyes closed and smiled while slowly nodding yes.

When we were done, I asked her what had happened. She told me that when I touched her shoulders, she felt a surge of energy and just about stood up out of the chair. I was really getting into this reiki thing, and I was feeling excited.

On our lunch break I noticed that the skin on my hands was starting to peel off as if I had a sunburn that had blistered. It wasn't painful by any means,

but it was obvious, and others noticed it as well. I thought it was interesting that we were sending healing energy through our hands and that now the skin on my hands was peeling away like blistered paint on an old barn door.

After lunch we had one more practice session with our partners. This time I performed the reiki on my partner first. I had decided that touching the person was more effective, so I decided I would place my hands on her again. I started by just holding her hand and shoulder, but soon found myself at her feet. The moment I touched her feet, I could taste dirt in my mouth. It reminded me of riding horses back in Texas as a kid. The next thing I knew I was asking my partner if she rode horses. She immediately opened her eyes and looked at me and said, "Why did you just ask me that?"

I explained, "As soon as I touched your feet I could taste dirt in my mouth, like I was riding a horse and tasting the dust in the air from the rider in front of me."

When we finished our session, she told me that she had grown up on a farm and had been riding horses her entire life. She went on to say that she had sold her farm in the States and all of her horses to move to Costa Rica a few years back. She gave me a hug and thanked me for the memory.

I went home even more excited about reiki and the gifts it had brought into my life. My hands continued to peel for the rest of the week, and for the first time I was starting to believe that maybe the people who were telling me I was a healer were right. I felt I was healing myself, putting myself and my life back together again.

CHAPTER 15

Grasshopper

After a few months of venturing deeper into shamanism, my friend Sabina told me that her ex-husband's brother was a powerful healer and that he was coming to Costa Rica. Sabina said, "When we found out Kent was coming, my ex and I immediately thought of you. He called Kent in California to ask if he would be willing to work with you, but Kent's wife answered the phone and said he had just gone into his meditation room and wouldn't be done for several hours."

She continued excitedly, "But after only a few minutes, my phone rang, and my ex answered it. Kent, even before hearing our question, said, 'Tell the guy you want me to work on that I'll be there in two weeks – and that I will see him.' My ex asked him, 'But how did you know I wanted you to work on this guy? I didn't tell your wife why I was calling!' Kent explained to him, 'When I started my meditation, my guides came to me and said that you would be calling on behalf of a friend who needed healing in Costa Rica and that I should get up now and call you to agree to the healing.' I've known Kent for years and was still shocked!"

Sabina told me this story a week or so before Kent came to Costa Rica. I was beginning to see changes in myself; my intuition was telling me that these coincidences were synchronicities. No longer was my mind so eager to call "bullshit" on the stories that people related to me about healing and the spiritual realm.

On the day of my appointment with Kent the healer, we were all invited to a big community dinner at Sabina's farm. I was to come up early and receive the healing before the other guests arrived. I drove up to the farm with my family and Erin's friend.

When we arrived we were greeted by Sabina's ex. He informed us that Sabina was ill and sleeping, and that his brother was running a little late. I said, "Hey, thanks so much for setting this all up with your brother."

"Don't thank me yet; you have no idea what you're in for!" he exclaimed. "My brother just needs you to fill out a medical release form before he can work on you."

Now I was starting to feel a little nervous. I had never been asked to fill out a medical release form to see a healer. I finished up the form, and just as my nerves were getting the best of me, Kent arrived.

Kent was an average-sized guy with a shaved head and regular clothes – nothing fancy or ceremonial. He didn't have any beads or crystals around his neck. He was just like me – a regular guy. When he opened his mouth, a loud, commanding, yet loving voice struck my ears with tidal force. He introduced himself to me and then looked at my release form. He sat down and asked me if I knew anything about numerology. When I said no he proceeded to show me how it worked and used my birthdate to determine what my soul path was.

When Kent finished, he asked, "Do strangers come to you and tell you about their lives? If so, are they just talking or are they telling you about deep, dark secrets and painful experiences?"

I asked, "How do you know that people do that to me all the time?"

He explained, "It's in the cosmos – a trait bred into you from birth. It's on your soul path and what you came here to do."

"What do you mean it's what I came here to do?"

"Hey, Grasshopper, you have a lot to learn about yourself. You're a healer, Man! Don't you know that about yourself by now?"

"All the shamans, psychics, and healers I've seen tell me that I'm a healer, but I don't understand how or what I'm supposed to be doing or healing. I'm still trying to heal myself!"

He erupted into his loud, reverberating laugh and stared into my eyes. Then he said, "You're afraid, and you don't believe in yourself. You question everything too much, and you want to know what's going on and why. Well, guess what, Grasshopper; you're not going to be able to figure this one out. You just have to claim it and accept your role." He went on to say, "Like it or not, people are going to keep coming to you, and they will start coming more frequently and in greater numbers. You can't stop it. You chose to do this work when you committed to healing yourself." Then he stood up and declared, "We're ready now. Let's go into the next room and do this!"

We entered the dark, bamboo-paneled room, and there was an air mattress on the floor. I gave him an anxious glance and apologized. "I'm sorry, but I can't get on the floor by myself."

His head snapped around and he peered deep into my soul and said, "Don't you fucking apologize to me! You didn't do anything wrong, and there is nothing wrong with needing some help! I've been helping people up and down for years. I can handle you, Grasshopper."

I gave him my walker and he sat me down on his knee and then laid me on the air mattress. He asked if I was comfortable and then reached back to grab his bag. He took three things out of the bag. The first was a small cloth that he laid over my stomach. The second was a strange stone from Machu Picchu with three rounded nodes on it. The last item was a large piece of black obsidian from Mt. Shasta.

Kent explained that he would be using the cloth in the healing and placing his hand on the cloth to work on my body. He also told me the significance and power behind the stone and the obsidian. He said, "When I'm working on you, if the pain gets too intense I want you to squeeze those stones and focus your attention on them. Okay, Grasshopper?"

Once I was settled in with the stones, he handed me a meditation mask to block out the lights of the room and help me stay focused. He instructed me to take the deepest breath I could and hold it while he pushed on my stomach and other areas of my body. "Once I release you from a position, I want you to release the air as if you just swam up from the ocean floor. Don't let the breath out while I'm working on you, understand?"

As I lay back into the air mattress, I could feel the hard wood floor underneath me. I put on the mask and felt the cloth being placed over my stomach. I had the obsidian in my right hand and the other stone in my left hand. It was as black as the ocean floor under my mask, and I had no idea what was about to happen to me.

I took my first deep breath on command and held it as directed until told to release and breathe deeply. Each time I held my breath and Kent pushed his hands into my stomach, it felt as if his hands were passing through the cloth and massaging or squeezing my internal organs.

The first thing I noticed after about ten minutes was that I could no longer feel the hard wood floor under my back. I was beginning to feel as if I was floating with my back just lightly touching the mattress. The next thing I encountered were smells from my childhood filling the room – the fragrances of my past. These smells made me think of my grandparents, and then my parents, respectively.

I asked, "Do you smell that?"

"Yeah, I smell it! It's coming out of you. These are the aromas of your past that you're releasing," he said.

Several minutes passed, and Kent's manipulations became painful. He began to cough and burp as more smells and past feelings rose to the surface. He asked me if I wanted to stop or keep going, and I said, "I can handle a little more if you can."

He laughed and said, "There you go, Grasshopper! I can hear the real you coming out now. These next few positions are going to hurt, but if you can hold on and hold your breath it would be really beneficial for you to do them."

"Let's do it; I'm ready!" I eagerly replied.

He then pressed his hands into my solar plexus for what felt like an eternity. When he released me and I had taken a deep breath, he asked, "What do you see?"

I was shocked because to my surprise I could see geometric patterns everywhere whether I opened my eyes or closed them under the mask. I was a little overwhelmed by how he always knew what was going on with me during the session, so I didn't say anything. He said louder, "Come on, Grasshopper. Don't get shy now! What do you see?"

"I don't know what I see. It looks like a bunch of geometric patterns, and they're everywhere I look. It looks like I'm tripping really hard on LSD."

"Good," he responded knowingly. "Okay, here we go again. Take a deep breath." This time he held the position even longer than the last and I felt like I was going to lose it. The pain was deep, and it felt like his hands were touching my spine – as if he had pushed his hands right through me. He released, and I gasped for air. "What do you see now?" he asked.

Once more the scene had changed right on cue. This time I was even more confused, because it took me a minute to figure it out. "I think I'm seeing stars, but they're different from the stars I'm used to seeing from earth! Now that I'm looking closer I can see that there is some kind of a line joining all the stars together, kind of like a map. Yeah, that's it. It's some kind of constellation or star map!" I shouted in stunned confusion.

"Yes, it is a star map. You must remember that you are a celestial being. It's a map of the places you've been in the universe! You see, you've become so grounded in this earth that you've forgotten where you come from. All your logical thinking and trying to figure things out has clouded your vision and kept you grounded here in this life, in your current situation. Do you understand?" he asked.

"Yeah," was all I could muster.

"Here we go, Grasshopper. Last one. I need you to hold tight and whatever you do, don't let your breath go. This one's gonna hurt."

This one's gonna hurt? Well, what about all the other ones? I thought to myself.

It was painful, and again seemed to stretch out longer than a line at Disneyland in July. I could feel my body begging me to slap his hands away and take that vital breath, but I held strong. I was squeezing the stones in my hands so hard that a small shard of obsidian broke off in my hand. As he released me, I spat and coughed while I struggled to catch my breath.

I noticed the scene had changed again. But this time it was so overwhelming that all I could do was cry. I felt warm tears damming up against the sides of the meditation mask. I wasn't actively crying as much as I couldn't stop the flow of tears. As the tears welled up, the mask gave way, and I felt my face and ears become wet with emotional release.

Then I heard that booming voice and the question, "What do you see now, Grasshopper?" I was so stunned by what I was seeing that I couldn't speak. Again I heard, "Come on, Grasshopper; it's okay. I know what you're seeing. I can see them, too. Just say it!" I opened and closed my eyes several times attempting to clear away the tears. It didn't matter if my eyes were opened or closed; the scene didn't change.

I finally found my voice, and with an unsteady stream of words I said, "I don't know what I'm seeing. I'm confused. I can see myself lying on the floor, but I'm looking down at myself from above as if I'm not in my body."

"Yeah. What else do you see?" he questioned further.

"I can see all kinds of beings that look like people, but they're much larger than me, and they're standing in a circle around me. The more I pull back from the scene the more of them I see, and more keep coming."

"What do they look like?" he asked.

As I tried to investigate further, I noticed that I was back in my body again, now looking up at these massive beings. "I don't know. It's hard to tell. I can see their feet, legs, hands, and bodies, but as I probe higher and higher there is a light that is so bright that I can't make out their faces," I explained.

His last question to me was, "What do you think they are?"

I took a deep breath and let out a big sigh and blurted out, "I don't know, but I feel really good right now, like I'm floating on a cloud. And all I can think is that these are angels or spirits of some kind!"

I heard a chuckling response, "Very good, Grasshopper! Do you know why they're all here?"

"No," I admitted.

"They're here for you, to help you and support you on your journey. They want me to give you a message, but I don't understand what it means. They said to tell you that they have always been here with you, but that they have been waiting for you to become aware of their presence and eagerness to help you. They said that they always knew you would come to this point, but that you're early. Does that mean anything to you?"

I felt the tears welling up again, and I said, "Yeah, it does. You see, from the moment that I was diagnosed with muscular dystrophy, I've always had this feeling that one day, when I was ready, I would be healed. Now I understand that this wasn't just wishful thinking; it was a knowing, a deep-seated truth that comes from the essence of who I really am. I finally understand that I can't do it on my own. And it feels great to know that I'm not alone on my mission."

"Hey, Grasshopper, I want you to know something, too. In the over twenty years that I've been doing this work, I've never seen so many spirits gathered in support around a single person. You are loved and supported, and don't you ever forget that." Then he asked, "How do you feel? Are you ready to get up and have some dinner with your family and friends?"

"I think so," I said.

"Now before you take off the mask and I turn on the light, I want you to understand that things may look different than they did before we started. Don't be scared; everything is okay. Are you ready to get up now?" he asked again.

I took off my mask, and Kent turned on the light and reached out his hand to help me up. When my eyes met his I felt a cold rush of confusion. His eyes were blacker than the deepest corners of the universe. I pulled my hand back in hesitation and he said, "Don't be afraid, Grasshopper. Everything is okay. Take my hand."

I grabbed his hand and in a flash I was on the couch sitting next to him. I gestured towards the walker and asked, "Can you hand me that stupid thing so I can get up?"

He grabbed the walker, set it down in front of me, peered into my eyes with his black-hole expression, and said, "Stop fucking talking like that and beating yourself up just because you need help. Didn't you learn anything here tonight, Grasshopper? The sooner you love and accept this walker as a tool and a part of your life, the sooner it will stop being a burden to your life."

"I understand. I get it," I said.

When I stood up, he gave me a huge hug and said, "I love you, Grasshopper. You're going to be fine. But if you start talking that negative shit to yourself again you're gonna see me. I'll be there in your head saying, 'Shut the fuck up. Stop talking to yourself that way and change your attitude.' Believe me; you'll hear me and I'll see you. What you need to do right now is love and forgive yourself. Do you understand?"

After that he opened the door and we emerged into a room full of people waiting for us so that we could all eat. Erin seemed to float across the room. As she got closer I noticed a strange look on her face. She stopped right in front of me and asked, "Are you okay? You look different. Your face and skin look all fuzzy like you're vibrating!" She reached out to touch my cheek, and I noticed that she looked out of focus to me, too – as if there were a halo around her. As her hand landed lightly on my face, everything snapped back into focus and I was officially back in reality.

After dinner, as the night lingered on, Erin and her friend questioned me about what had happened during the healing. They had both noticed Kent's eyes completely black when he came out of the room, which startled them, too. I explained in detail everything we had done. I told them how he called me Grasshopper and kept telling me to stop fucking apologizing for my situation and needing help and so on.

As the night came to a close, we all loaded up in the car for the long haul home. During the drive I kept going over my experience, and at some point Erin turned and said, "At first when you started telling me about Kent and the way he was talking to you, I thought he sounded like a jerk. But now after hearing your voice and seeing the change in you, I think that sometimes people need to hear harsh words spoken with loving intent in order to be shaken up and recognize what they are doing to themselves with their negative attitudes. He may not have been all warm, lovey, and huggy, but you're not either, and you don't really like all that fake huggy stuff anyway. I think he was the perfect match for you because he's so much like you and could relate to you."

She was right. Kent was just the loving kick-in-the-ass I needed on my journey at that time. He shook me just hard enough for me to realize that I wasn't broken. He also helped me find a deeper connection with my spiritual family, who came out that night to show their limitless support and unfathomable love for me.

That night I gained the clarity I needed to start forgiving myself. It took time and effort, but the more I let go and forgave others, the easier it became to forgive myself.

CHAPTER 16

Unmasked

> *"All that we are is the result of what we have thought. If a man speaks or acts with an evil thought, pain follows him. If a man speaks or acts with a pure thought, happiness follows him, like a shadow that never leaves him."*
>
> —*Buddha*

One day my friend and reiki instructor, Victoria, introduced me to a man very small in stature with silvery hair and a long wizard's beard to match. His name was Don, and he seemed to peer into my eyes and see right through me. He knew things about me and was able to recognize the road map of emotional scars in my eyes. He told me that his ability or "vision" came from years of working with his own shadow as well as helping clients work on theirs.

I had no idea what he was talking about. He went on to say, "People hide from themselves and others. They hide the things that they don't like about their lives – like fear, pain, and trauma – in their *shadow self* so that it isn't obvious on the surface. Then they put on a mask to cover their pain and show a false representation of themselves to the world. These masks come in many forms, and we can change our masks depending on the situations that arise. When people feel deep emotional pain from their past, they put on a mask and push their feelings away into their shadow, not realizing that the shadow follows them everywhere they go."

I thought about this analogy. Just as our physical shadows change, distort, and misrepresent us over the course of the day, our emotional shadows distort and misrepresent who we are and how we see ourselves in our world. These illusions cause strain in our everyday lives, at work, in our relationships, in our finances, and in practically every aspect of our lives. It's not until we embrace our shadows and examine what we are hiding from ourselves that we can begin to heal and forgive our shadow selves.

Don explained to me that our physical shadows are helpful to us in knowing our positions and orientations. Our emotional shadows are also there to help guide us, revealing our judgments, anxieties, fears, and unsorted pasts. In other words, our shadow selves aren't wrong or bad; they're here to lovingly help us remember the issues that we've attempted to push down and resist. Our shadow selves help us keep track of the things in our lives that we need to forgive and release so that we can shine brightly and show who we really are.

More than intrigued, I decided to attend Don's shadow workshop. The workshop began early in the morning, and we started by introducing ourselves to one another. The group was small – three women and four men, including myself. I was the youngest of the group; everyone else was at least fifteen years older than I. I thought to myself that it would be interesting to learn about the perspectives of people who were a generation removed from my way of thinking.

After our introductions we began the first exercise. We all stood in a circle looking at each other, and Don said, "I want y'all to look at all the people in this circle and walk over and put your hand on the shoulder of the person you trust the least, purely based on what you can observe only with your eyes."

I felt nervous, and this exercise felt bad to me. I was immediately being asked to make judgments about people I didn't know anything about other than their names and where they were from. My first thought was that nobody was going to pick me because I knew myself to be honest and trustworthy. I quickly settled on my choice: a tall, older man with a well-weathered face. He had shifty eyes that peered mostly at the ground and a long shock of silvery gray hair tied back loosely into a ponytail.

I was the first person to walk over and touch someone on the shoulder. Then I was amazed to find three more people from the group walking in our direction. I thought I had made the right choice, and that everyone could see the same things in this man that I had, until they stopped short of him and placed their hands on me!

My next thought was one of confusion and judgment, and I wondered, "How can all of these people be choosing me? I'm a good person, and they don't even know me yet!" I was desperately attempting to protect my fragile ego.

Don suddenly approached me from behind and in a rapid-fire voice he said to me, "I'm going to count to three, and I want you to look into the eyes of the person you just chose and say why you don't trust them." Before I could prepare my words he counted out, "One, two, three!"

I looked deep into the stranger's eyes, but as soon as I started to speak Don threw up a mirror between us, and all I could see was myself as I said, "I don't trust you because I don't even know who you are!"

I quickly understood the point of the exercise and felt the tears in my eyes welling up. I realized in that moment that we are all mirrors helping each other realize how we see ourselves. I understood that all of my thoughts and judgments about other people were caused by my own self-judgement. I also realized that the other people in the group had selected me as the person they trusted the least because I was the one in the group who trusted myself the least.

Don asked us to circle up again. This time Don said, "Now look across the circle and find the person you trust the most and go place your hand on their shoulder." This time I was more selective and careful about my choice. One of the men in our group was suffering from a severe case of cerebral palsy and could not control his body movements at all. I had seen the pain and anguish in his eyes the moment I had met him. I felt compelled to go and place my hand on his shoulder. Again Don walked up to me first and said, "When I count to three, look into your partner's eyes and tell him why you chose him. One, two, three!"

I looked into this man's shaky eyes, and as I started to speak the mirror was back, and all I could see was myself as I said, "I trust you the most because you're the most real person here. You're dealing with something that no one else can understand, and you can't hide it from the world. It's an obvious part of who you are." *Wow, that sounds strangely familiar*, I thought to myself.

The remainder of the three days was dedicated to deeper discovery of our shadow selves. We learned to bring these hidden parts of ourselves to the light to find the gifts they held for us. By the end of the workshop I had found that I didn't trust or believe in other people because I didn't trust or believe in myself. I found that I had been taught self-judgement, and that it came from my parents, my teachers, my coaches, and my culture at large telling me who and what I was. Yet *I* had not discovered who I truly

was. Everything I had believed about myself up to that point had been a consequence of judgments and cultural illusions.

In fact, these judgments were just faint, superficial impressions that my surroundings had branded on my character. By the end of the workshop I wondered who I really was, and would've been hard-pressed to describe myself to a stranger. Almost everything I had believed about myself to that point had been a grand illusion – nothing more than a list of criticisms and accusations disguised as my inner self.

I realized that I no longer had to play the role of the character that my culture had created. I didn't need to hide myself from the world and wear my burned badge of shame. By forgiving myself for believing those judgments to be true, I was able to forgive my parents, my past, and my culture.

When I deconstructed the walls that I had allowed my culture to build around me, I was able to lay a new foundation – a sort of launch pad devoid of structure and limits that would empower me to express myself and help my spirit take flight.

Eager and excited about my new insights, I went to visit my wise friend, Eugene. I wanted to tell him about my experiences in the shadow workshop because he'd always been an influential counselor to me in these times of great growth.

After an extended conversation about how we hide our true identities from ourselves and the world, he asked, "Why haven't you come by for a healing with me yet? I think you'd find it interesting. It's called SHEN energy healing."

Of course I was open and intrigued. "What's SHEN?"

He explained, "When I lived in Sri Lanka my shaman taught me about the chakras and energetic networks. SHEN stands for specific human energy nexus, and it has to do with alignment and opening the chakras to create healing and connection with spirit."

I asked, "So can this healing help me establish a better connection with my higher self and help me extract my essence?" He only smiled in reply. We set up a session, and I left feeling excited about exploring deeper into my inner self.

At our first session, I lay face down on a massage table and stated my intention to myself while Eugene was in the next room meditating and gathering his healing energy.

When he entered the room he put on some meditation music that was interwoven with whale songs.

As the healing session began I felt uncomfortable and found it hard to relax. I had known Eugene for a long time and knew that we had a very similar past regarding our parents and upbringing. I wanted to be a "good client" for him, but found that these thoughts were distracting me.

Finally, about twenty minutes into the session, I felt myself let go and saw a vision in my mind's eye. At first I couldn't make out what I was seeing. It looked like coiled ropes or braided cables swimming in a deep dark sea.

As I relaxed further into the experience, I looked closer and noticed that the coiled ropes were swimming up to the surface. When these coiled ropes shattered the surface they turned into huge whales expelling their hot, exhausted breath into the receptive sky. I watched as they repeatedly breached the surface, gasping for vital air as they celebrated their reconnection with life as a whale.

The pod of whales stayed on the surface for only a few minutes before they inhaled the life force of the earth and renewed their strange agreement with the sea. As they dove deep, these massive, majestic animals once again turned into twisted ropes, weaving their DNA back into a symbiosis with the sea.

This was a mind-blowing vision, but I understood the whales' message without a doubt. On the surface they took form and appeared as whales, an aspect and expression of the sea. But when they dove they returned to their essence, which was formless and nameless yet an integral part of the whole ocean.

I could see how we are the same as these whales. On the surface we have bodies and roles that we play in our world, which are nothing more than the expressions of what our culture and pasts have formed us to be. But below the surface we're connected with the whole of creation, and we just need to let go and deconstruct our perceived selves in order to weave our DNA into the tapestry of our true essence. Dissolving our surface selves allows us to make internal changes so that the new expressions of who we are become the reflections of our spirits.

When the session was over we walked out on the deck and looked out over the seascape in front of us. We saw a large pod of whales in the bay just below Eugene's house, and both laughed at the perfect synchronicity of their appearance.

In my next session with Eugene, I lay facing up on the massage table, intent on strengthening and building on my last healing. I had been preparing and meditating on my third-eye connection the prior week. After stating my intention and waiting while Eugene meditated in the next room, we were off. I could feel myself relaxing into a deep, meditative state from the start. Yet all I could see was darkness. The more I relaxed, the blacker it became, until finally I saw a flicker of light in my mind's eye. I was now accustomed to the visions in shamanic journeying, but this was strangely different. It looked like a spider or something crawling on a web in front of a bright light. But this light felt familiar, and it lacked the heat associated with the sun.

I concentrated on the light, but nothing more came of it as our session came to a close. I told Eugene about the "spider" and how the vision felt different, confusing, and unresolved. He had a strange look on his face, so I asked, "What's up? What do you think is going on?"

He responded, "When I was working on you I saw what looked like a string or something coming out of the right side of your head. I moved up to your head and concentrated on energetically pulling it out of your body. When I did, I felt a dark presence that didn't want to leave. When I asked it to go, a snake emerged from your stomach. It turned and faced me, staring into my eyes. I commanded it to go and release you from its constrictive grasp and aggressive influence. It immediately left and returned to where it had come from, and I moved to your stomach to ensure that it was gone. As I continued to focus my energy I saw a slithery stream of smoke exiting out of the left side of your head, and I knew the snake had gone."

I just stood there wide-eyed at his account. I felt lighter and more clearheaded than I had felt in many years, and I felt a slight tingle of joy and contentment with my life for maybe the first time ever. I knew from my shamanic practices that the snake represents transformation. I felt like a new person was emerging and shedding the tight, constrictive skin of my past.

By our third session I was feeling relaxed and focused. I kept my intention the same, as I had yet to achieve my goal of opening my third eye. Eugene, as always, began by meditating in the adjacent room. When he came in, I was on the massage table smiling, calmly excited about our time together.

He put on the music and began with the healing, and this time there was no delay before the flickering light appeared in my mind's eye. I decided to investigate the light and the "spider" further. As

I took a closer look, I could see that the light was getting brighter and the flicker of the image was intensifying. There was something other than the spider struggling to free itself from the cobwebs that entangled it. The flickering light grew more and more intense until, without warning, the last web strand snapped and light came flooding in.

At first the light was so bright that I couldn't see anything. As I lay there basking in this internal light, I remembered the healing ceremony with Kent, when the spirits appeared and I couldn't see their faces. Just as that thought entered my mind, an eye appeared in front of the light. I was elated and astonished to find that the eye that I was now staring into was my own familiar green eye. Then it dawned on me that I was gazing into my third eye, and that my higher self was a part of me. I was shocked to see that my third eye was a direct representation of my physical eyes.

Our session came to an end, and we walked out on the deck to discuss what had transpired, as usual. Eugene asked, "What are you smiling about?"

"I just had a crazy time in there, so thanks for your part. All three sessions I have been concentrating on my third eye, and today, Boom! It opened. And I was shocked to find that it was my eye, fully open, looking right back at me."

Through his laughter he said, "Well, whose eye did you think it was going to be? A lot of people think that your higher self, or third eye vision, is someone or somewhere outside of you, and that is a limiting belief. You need to claim your power and believe in yourself. It's you creating all of these changes in your life, with the help of your higher self, which is just another aspect of you. Claim your knowledge and insight, claim your third eye vision, because it's not outside of you. It is your essence shining through to the surface, weaving itself into your daily life and changing your perception of the things that you believe about yourself."

CHAPTER 17

Find Your Smile

"When angels visit us, we do not hear the rustle of wings, nor feel the feathery touch of the breast of a dove; but we know their presence by the love they create in our hearts."

—*Anonymous*

One afternoon while visiting Sabina, a tall, long-haired German man covered in tattoos from his neck to his feet came driving up the dusty road. She was excited for me to meet this man, as she had spoken to me about him and his healing modality over the last few months.

She introduced us, and I noticed as we made eye contact that he was shooting me that familiar, deep stare as he investigated my eyes. When healers I had met before had done this, it had made me feel self-conscious, but now I had a better understanding of what it was they were doing in that brief moment, so I relaxed and allowed him to go deep.

When he had connected with me in this way, he just gave me a knowing smile and said with a gruff German accent, "I'm Uli. Nice to meet you."

I smiled back and said, "Hey, I'm Jeff. Nice to meet you, Bro."

He wasted no time, but directly dove right into my personal, private world and said, "You were in the military and something went wrong while you were there, right? You've been angry about this and other painful things from your past for a very long time. Because of this rage, you have lost your smile. Because of this anger, you don't want to forgive even though you know how."

I cut my gaze over to Sabina and grinned, knowing that she hadn't told him anything about me before our introduction that day. We spoke for a while longer and then he offered to come to my house and facilitate a healing session with my family and friends. We exchanged info, and before he left he said to me, "I know it has been tough, your life, but after our session you will find your smile."

"That sounds nice. I mean, I like the idea of smiling if there's something to smile about," I said, flashing him a little smirk.

A few days later I called and made arrangements for Uli to come to my home and work with me, my family, and three of our friends. He arrived at our house just as the sun was setting and the seasonal warm evening rains began to fall. Everyone in the house was lit with wonder and curiosity as we greeted our guest at the door. Uli came in and immediately introduced himself to everyone with a sincere smile followed by a warm hug.

After he unloaded his car and set up the living room with candles and photos with angelic themes, Uli walked around the house performing an energy-balancing ceremony. He worked through all the rooms of the house, and when he felt the energy was in balance we all congregated in the living room with gleeful anticipation. I could feel the energy and excitement in the room growing.

Uli explained the process of *divine alignment* and said, "What we will be doing here tonight is asking

your angels to enter into your body and spiritually or energetically align your chakras. As an effect of this, your hips, shoulders, and spine will be physically straightened. This straightening occurs because you're allowing your body to release judgment while inviting angels to move you into alignment with your spirit. Since your angels never leave you, this alignment will stay with your current body for the rest of your physical life."

By the end of his explanation, I noticed that my friends John and Dan were giving me funny looks. Then John leaned towards me and whispered, "You don't really believe in all this crap, do you?"

I smiled and said, "I do believe in all this crap, and the sooner you decide to suspend your disbelief, the sooner you'll invite spirit into your life. I don't know how all of this stuff works, John, but I was just like you before I realized that if I want to see miracles manifest in my life, I need to unfold my belief in the miraculous. I had to stop judging things I didn't understand about spirit and start questioning the physical things that I believed to be true."

Just as I finished my quiet conversation with John, Uli asked everyone, "Who here already believes in angels, and do you talk with your angels?" He looked at me, pointed with a grin, and said, "Jeff believes. I can see his angels all around him jumping and laughing, telling me he believes and that he even talks to them. So tell everyone – is this true, Jeff?"

I just grinned and nodded my head as my friends John and Dan cut their eyes towards me in wavering disbelief. Erin and my kids were the next ones in the group to admit to believing in angels, followed by Dan's wife, Holly.

Uli laughed and then told each person in the room how many angels they had with them. He told us our angels were excited that we were going to allow them to actively and directly help us with our physical lives.

When Uli stopped chuckling he said, "This ceremony tonight is to invite your angels into your life so they can physically help and assist you. Because they're here to help on the physical plane, you will see physical changes immediately happen to each and every one of your bodies tonight." He explained further, "I will be measuring each person's shoulders, hips, and feet and checking your spine to see if it is straight. I will measure your legs and mark the heel of the longer leg across from where the shorter one ends due to misalignment. Then I will call your angels into your body to perform the straightening. Afterward everyone will come forward and immediately witness the physical changes in your body, which only takes a minute or two. You'll see that no matter how far out of alignment anyone here is, it will be corrected in the moment."

With that, he asked for his first volunteer, and Erin quickly shot her hand up in the air. Uli smiled and motioned Erin towards the massage table. As she approached, Uli looked her in the eyes and asked if she was ready to start. She smiled and nodded. He stopped her in the center of the room, took out his yardstick, and measured her spine, showing all of us the differences in alignment on either side of her body. She then lay face down on the table and he used the yardstick to measure the difference in the length of her legs.

Everyone in the group came up to the table to observe the marks and the difference in Erin's two legs. We could clearly see that her left leg extended about a half inch beyond her right leg. Everyone returned to their seats and Uli began to pray in German for Erin's angels to enter her body and help her align with spirit.

After the prayer he used his hands to guide and direct the energy from her head down through her body and out through her feet. The process took about two minutes from start to finish, and when Uli was done he asked everyone to come and see Erin's new alignment. We approached, not knowing what to expect, and sure enough when he brought her heels together her legs were exactly the same length. Then Erin stood up in front of the room and Uli took out his yardstick to demonstrate how Erin's body was straight and in balance.

John and Dan looked at me silently with wide eyes. Their disbelief was gone, and a look of confounded interest had replaced it.

When we all returned to our seats, Uli sprinkled oil in his palms and rubbed them together, gathering energy and directing it into a "light shower" over the top of Erin's head. An instant smile gleamed across her face as he kept his hands above her, directing the energy down through the crown of her head.

Still glowing from the light shower, Erin came and sat next to me on the couch and declared, "That was awesome!" With her endorsement our shy friend Holly jumped to her feet and shouted, "I'm next!"

Uli repeated the same measurements and rituals on Holly. We all observed the difference in the length of her legs and in her alignment before and after. To no one's surprise, she was in perfect alignment.

But to our surprise, Holly began to cry uncontrollably during her light shower. Uli told her to let go; to let the tears flow and heal her troubled mind. He told her that he could see her difficult life and past lives. He said a few things privately in her ear, and she began to cry even harder as she vigorously nodded her head in agreement with his words. He asked her if she was ready to release her past, and she nodded. He came around to the front of her, placed his right hand on her chest for a moment, and then quickly drew it away as if pulling something energetic out of her. She immediately stopped crying and opened her eyes with the biggest smile that I'd ever seen her wear. Uli said, "You're free now. Go and live in the light of who you are now in this life."

Holly turned and gave Uli a big hug and came to sit down by her husband, Dan, who was the first to notice that Holly looked different. He said to me, "Dude, look at Holly's face and eyes. She looks younger, and her eyes have never looked so clear and pure." I looked over at her, and it was true. She

looked ten years younger, and her eyes bore the same joy as that of the smile on her face.

After Holly's visibly moving experience, John jumped up eager to be the next beneficiary of this angelic energy. By now his disbelief had been dismissed by the tidal wave of loving energy that was lifting all our souls to a higher frequency.

I was the last of the adults to go, and was a little concerned about how the screws and metal plates in my pelvis would be affected by the alignment. Uli told me that everything would be fine and that if anyone understood what my body could handle, it would be my angels. He began to take measurements, and then helped me onto the table where I lay down so he could measure my legs. I was shocked to find out that my right leg was over an inch shorter than my left. Uli leaned over and asked me if I was ready for the alignment. I said, "Yes!"

As he began, I could feel warm energy moving through my body. The top of my head and my face felt flushed, and there was a euphoric, fluttering feeling that moved down through my body in pulsating waves. Just as I thought that I couldn't possibly feel any more comfortable, warm, and relaxed, Uli called everyone up to see the results.

My body had miraculously shifted so that my legs were the same length.

During my light shower Uli said, "Your angels want you to relax and let go of your concerns about your perceived limitations." He paused, seeming to concentrate on a thought, and then continued, "You're fulfilling your mission in this life through firsthand experiences and sharing your knowledge with others. They want you to let go of thinking that you would be more helpful and useful if you didn't have this disease, and instead pass your understanding of pain and personal healing on to others."

My two sons were the last ones to go, and they were excited to jump up on the massage table and receive their alignments. When Uli measured my youngest son, Kai, his right leg was longer than his left. When he had measured everyone else, it had been the other way around. He stopped and explained to us that only about 10 percent of people in the world have a right leg longer than the left, and that these people are here to carry out very specific missions in life. He explained that these people are born with a strong soul connection and a strong sense of purpose. Then he tickled Kai a little and finished up with him.

Daegan's right leg was also longer than his left. The moment Uli discovered this, he shot a piercing glance at me and said, "You know why these two sons of yours have the right leg longer than the left, don't you?"

I wasn't expecting his question, and I didn't know what to say, so I just repeated the first words that came to my mind: "They're here to help me?"

"That's right, Man! You are so supported by your angels that you even have the physical incarnation of angelic help on your side manifested through your children."

I was overwhelmed by the idea that I had been gifted two spiritual warriors to lend me the strength and fortitude to overcome life's challenges through their examples of acceptance and love. I was taken aback when I realized that my children had always accepted me and loved me unconditionally even when I wasn't capable of loving myself. Furthermore, there was nothing wrong with me, and in their innocent eyes, nothing to forgive me for.

CHAPTER 18

Harmony

Six years later, after traveling down the long, tangled road of mental, physical, and spiritual recovery, I went back to Texas to visit the "lion's den." While excited to see my family and friends, this trip also meant staying with my lifelong nemesis and the most challenging of people, Dad.

Why did I choose to throw myself into the fire? It's easy to convince yourself that you've healed and changed your life when you're a thousand miles away from the people, pain, and memories that caused your overwhelming gloom. It's quite another thing to test and witness these changes in a visceral way.

On the surface nothing had changed. I still had muscular dystrophy, I still needed a walker to get around, and Dad was still an angry, unhappy, miserable guy. The difference was that now I didn't carry the same burdens. During my visit, the usual nasty, hurtful things were said and done. But I was able to see through the hateful mask Dad used to hide the pain, and forgive him in the moment. I realized that he only hated the perception of himself in the world and never allowed himself to explore the past and forgive his parents. This realization shifted my view of Dad, and I felt compassion, knowing that he may never change.

I felt sadness for him, too, because deep down I love Dad. I wished that he would come to understand the things I had learned on my journey. I knew then that I had truly forgiven myself, and consequently Dad. Sometimes gifts come in broken, battered packages that nobody wants. If you try hard enough, you can unwrap the purpose and joy they hold. Most of the time the way he delivered his messages was abusive and painfully wrong, but through his actions Dad made me tough, resilient, and strong. I quietly thanked Dad for the gifts he had given me; he had created a warrior who never gave up on himself, even when there seemed to be no hope.

HARMONY

When I started writing this book, I didn't know what I was doing. I only felt the need to purge my pain and try to help others through my story. I wanted to share the experiences that changed my life in profound and unforeseen ways. While the words poured out, I started to see a pattern of holding on to the past and not wanting to let go of who I thought I was. On my journey I noticed that the healers on my path were telling me to forgive, and I learned that I hadn't known how to forgive people and past grievances.

I went through the process of saying aloud, "I forgive so and so for such and such." But the next time I interacted with the person, and saw they hadn't changed, I felt even more frustration, which exposed my lack of true forgiveness.

After seeing this pattern repeated several times in my story, I went deeper into meditation and self-discovery. I started to view my life as a learning experience and an opportunity to share my process and help people achieve the previously unattainable. The process takes patience, practice, and time, but the journey is just as satisfying as the reward. There is no quick fix, and no one can do it for you.

1. Accept Your Present Life

I was full of rage because I refused to accept my present life. I had to learn how to accept myself completely – as I was in the moment, and not wish for a future in which I had already changed myself and had a "better life." I had to accept the broken, angry, diseased person who hated his life. In other words, I had to be *who* I was in the moment; I had to be *where* I was in the moment. I also had to look and listen without boundaries or judgments. While allowing my friends and the healers to relay their masterful lessons to me, I was forced to reflect on how I spoke to and thought of myself.

By not accepting where I was, I had empowered the negative thoughts and allowed them to manifest as rage and judgment towards everyone around me. I had become a battle-tested warrior, unwilling to surrender even though the war was over. When I began to accept my state of disease and frustration, I could see that I had allowed the very things I despised to rule my life.

2. Surrender to the Past

Once I was able to accept myself and my current way of thinking, my inner warrior took off his armor of aggression and surrendered to what was. I could see that I had been fighting against my past, waging a mental war against all of the negative memories and hurtful experiences. The hardest part was admitting to myself that these battles had ended long ago yet I had continued to fight against my childhood and things that had happened years and even decades before. I realized that surrender did not mean giving up; it meant a chance for survival. I couldn't change the course of these long-lost battles or the people I fought against. Raising the white flag of surrender allowed me to gain an understanding of why certain people and experiences had come into my life.

3. Understand the Purpose

My understanding grew beyond myself and my narrow, one-sided view of the world. Instead of feeling sorry for myself and regretting the things others had done to me, I tried to understand their

circumstances, as many people are products of their cultural upbringing and unable to control their programmed responses. This perspective helped me see that others were just reacting to me based on their own unaccepted pasts, which brought me clarity about why people do harmful things to each other. I began to understand why certain things had happened to me and that they would continue to happen in the same way until I discovered the hidden lessons in them and their purpose in my life.

4. Forgive Others

Letting go is true forgiveness; it allows you to become unattached and free to create something new in the space once filled with resentment and discontent. Holding on to anger only creates more chaos and confusion. When I discovered the secret of forgiveness, I realized that my life was changing right before my eyes. I found my "inner sage" and learned that he dwells in the house of forgiveness. I learned that I could only forgive the things I had accepted, and that I could only surrender after removing the armor of anger. True understanding of why things happen can only come from accepting, not judging, others. Once I had accepted and understood my past, I was able to let it go and find forgiveness.

5. Love Yourself

The more I let go of the past and accepted my present, the more I was able to forgive and love myself for holding on. This was the most important and most difficult step of all. As I released myself from the mental cage of anger and resentment, I found myself standing free, unhindered by painful memories and past grievances. Forgiveness of others allowed me to love more openly and find a place I call "forgiveness in the moment." I became addicted to the feeling of bliss created by acceptance and forgiveness, and realized that I needed to direct these feelings towards myself as well as others. I started this journey with the intention of healing myself and consequently learned how to love myself.

6. Harmonize and Realize

When we harmonize our thoughts, feelings, and emotions in love, we realize our dreams; our harmony becomes reality. It's nothing more than a choice. When our feelings and emotions are discordant, the only way to create a new reality is through forgiveness. By choosing to live in the power of love and forgiveness, we create harmony in our lives. This harmony attracts like-minded people and experiences that reinforce the feelings of love and abundance at play in our lives. In time, as our loving thoughts, feelings, and emotions continue to harmonize, we realize the life we have desired.

The process of acceptance, surrender, and understanding allows us to forgive others and love ourselves so we can find harmony and change our current situations. I've witnessed these miracles in my life. Blame was transformed into blessings, judgment was smiled upon in jest, and anger gave way to a passion for sharing my experience of forgiveness and love with others. By detaching from the opinions and judgments of others and discovering who I truly was, I was able to create a new vibration and attract like-minded people who helped and supported me along the way. They helped me shift my perspective and create a new reality.

At this point on my journey I'm able to see the transformation from outer rage to inner sage. It required dedication. It began with the humble belief that I could change my outer world by changing my inner perceptions. Instead of operating as a victim who suffers from hardships and disease, I now project myself as a strong, resilient person who is able to overcome any obstacle. Although I had a lot of help along the way, I alone had to make the decision to transform my life. I discovered the true healer on my journey… I just never expected it would be me!

ACKNOWLEDGMENTS

I'd like to thank my wife, Erin Anthony, for helping me find my way – not just through this book, but back to myself. Without her support (and occasional kick in the ass) none of this would have been possible. She saw something in me that I had lost sight of a long time ago. I love you! My deepest gratitude to my sons, Daegan and Kai, for being my motivation and inspiration in life. Thanks to my parents for making me strong and resilient enough to face my challenges and overcome.

Transforming a book from good to great takes a team effort and this wouldn't have been possible without the passionate contributions of my editors, Allison Saia and Gwen Hoffnagle, publishing assistant Carrie Jareed, cover artist Brian Sylvester, and the team at Transformation Books.

I would also like to recognize the help and support of the following people throughout this process: Monk and Mona, Rob and Aubree Brown, Kevin Carpenter, Erik and Nicole Blaker, Matt and Laraina Heeler, Dylan and Anna Hunt, Jennifer Smith, Josh and Tina Alas, Tim Rath, Marco Gutierrez, and Ryan Cornelius.

ABOUT THE AUTHOR

After overcoming a lifetime of hardships, and learning to withstand those he cannot change, author Jeff Anthony has become a great resource for people who are facing their own challenges. His personal experiences with abuse, addiction, and physical disability allow him to empathize with others and offer useful, realistic advice. Although everyone's  journey in life is unique, people from all backgrounds are inspired by Jeff's story and guided by his powerful message of forgiveness and acceptance.

In his first book, *Cosmic Wizard*, Jeff reveals even his darkest moments of anger and depression followed by uplifting twists as he shows us the way out. Jeff says, "Writing this book was a roller–coaster ride of emotions. I had to examine my past and let go of the shame and embarrassment I felt about exposing my choices and mistakes. It was not easy, but in order to help others I had to be brutally honest with myself."

Jeff's greatest passion is helping others. He has discovered that speaking honestly about his life causes others to open up about their own lives. This allows him to offer realistic solutions aimed at the root of the problem. While he attempts to guide others and encourage people to change their perspectives, Jeff believes that we all have the ability to help ourselves, and his ultimate goal is to empower others with this belief.

Individuals and groups seeking Jeff's inspirational message can contact him through his website: *www.journeytoinnersage.com.*

www.ingramcontent.com/pod-product-compliance
Lightning Source LLC
Chambersburg PA
CBHW021144080526
44588CB00008B/205